Basic Business Statistics

A Casebook

Springer

New York
Berlin
Heidelberg
Barcelona
Budapest
Hong Kong
London
Milan
Paris
Santa Clara
Singapore
Tokyo

Basic Business Statistics

A Casebook

Dean P. Foster
Robert A. Stine
Richard P. Waterman
University of Pennsylvania
Wharton School

Springer

Dean P. Foster
Robert A. Stine
Richard P. Waterman
Department of Statistics
Wharton School
University of Pennsylvania
Philadelphia, PA 19104
USA

Library of Congress Cataloging-in-Publication Data
Foster, Dean P.
    Basic business statistics : a casebook / Dean P. Foster, Robert A.
Stine, Richard P. Waterman.
      p.   cm.
    Includes index.
    ISBN 0-387-98354-6 (softcover : alk. paper)
    1. Commercial statistics.   2. Commercial statistics — Case studies.
 I. Stine, Robert A. II. Waterman, Richard P. III. Title.
HF1017.F67 1998
519.5 — dc21   97-39225

Printed on acid-free paper.

Minitab is a registered trademark of Minitab, Inc.

Production managed by Timothy Taylor; manufacturing supervised by Jeffrey Taub.
Camera-ready copy prepared from the authors' WordPerfect files.
Printed and bound by Maple-Vail Book Manufacturing Group, York, PA.
Printed in the United States of America.

9 8 7 6 5 4 3 2 1

ISBN 0-387-98354-6 Springer-Verlag New York Berlin Heidelberg SPIN 10646874

Preface

Statistics is seldom the most eagerly anticipated course of a business student. It typically has the reputation of being a boring, complicated, and confusing mix of mathematical formulas and computers. Our goal in writing this casebook and the companion volume (*Business Analysis Using Regression*) was to change that impression by showing how statistics yields insights and answers interesting business questions. Rather than dwell on underlying formulas, we show how to use statistics to answer questions. Each case study begins with a business question and concludes with an answer to that question. Formulas appear only as needed to address the questions, and we focus on the insights into the problem provided by the mathematics. The mathematics serves a purpose.

The material in this casebook is organized into 11 "classes" of related case studies that develop a single, key idea of statistics. The analysis of data using statistics is seldom very straightforward, and each analysis has many nuances. Part of the appeal of statistics is this richness, this blending of substantive theories and mathematics. For newcomers, however, this blend is too rich, and they are easily overwhelmed and unable to sort out the important ideas from nuances. Although later cases in these notes suggest this complexity, we do not begin that way. Each class has one main idea, something big such as standard error. We begin a class by discussing an application chosen to motivate this key concept, and introduce the necessary terminology. All of the cases in that class explore and develop that idea, with perhaps a suggestion of the idea waiting in the next class. Time in the classroom is a limited commodity, and we use it to apply statistics rather than talk about statistics. We do the data analysis of these cases in class using a computer projection system. This allows us to explore tangents and gives students a chance to see the flow of data analysis. We use a supplemental textbook to fill voids in our coverage and to complete the development of underlying calculations and formulas. These casebooks remove much of the note-taking burden so that students can follow along without trying to draw plots or scribble down tables. That said, we have seen that students still seem to fill every margin with notes from class. The course seems to work. It has been very highly rated by MBA students, and some have even come to ask about majoring in statistics!

It would be easy to claim that you can use any statistics software with these casebooks, but that's not entirely true. Before we developed these notes, we needed to choose the software that we would use to do the analyses and generate the figures that appear in this book. The preferences of our students demanded that we needed something that ran on PCs and Macs; our own needs required that the software be able to handle large data sets, offer modern interactive graphics (plot linking, brushing), and include tools for the beginner up through logistic regression. JMP (whose student version is named JMP-IN) was the best fit to our criteria. Each of its analysis procedures includes a graph as part of the output, and even the student version allows an unlimited data set size (up to the capabilities of the computer). It's also very fast and was designed from the start with a graphical user interface. To top it off, the developers of JMP, led by John Sall at SAS, have been very responsive to our suggestions and have added crucial features that we needed. We're aware, though, that many will prefer to use another package, particularly Minitab. Minitab finished a close second to JMP in our comparisons of statistical software and is well-suited to accompany these notes. An appendix describes the commands from the student version of Minitab that provide the needed functionality.

A mixture of real and simulated data are used in the cases. We often use simulated or artificial data when we want to focus on a particular technique or issue. Real data are seldom so simple and typically have numerous nuances that distract from the point being made. The resulting analysis can become so convoluted that everyone tends to get lost. The data for the included assignments were used recently when we taught this course (we have to change the assignments annually). You may want to require these or modify them to suit your emphasis. All of the data sets used in these examples (in both JMP and ASCII formats) are available over the Internet from either StatLib (http://lib.stat.cmu.edu) or our departmental web site (http://www-stat.wharton.upenn.edu).

A Brief Overview of the Cases

We have used the material in this book as the lecture notes for an intensive 3-week "pre-term" course in the MBA program at Wharton. This course is taken by virtually all incoming MBA students prior to the start of the usual semester. In many ways, the course is intended to be a leveling experience, bringing students to a common level of preparation so that all are prepared to begin the fall semester with regression analysis. The pace (3 or 4 classes a week) of the Wharton pre-term and the fact that this course is not graded require that we make the material as interesting and engaging as possible. The first 7 lectures of our course are each 2 hours long, and the remaining 4 last 1.5 hours. Generally, though, there is more material in these notes than can be adequately covered in even the 2-hour classes. At a minimum, you will want to cover the first example for each class since this example generally introduces the methods with more discussion; later examples for each class offer repetition and explore tangential (important, but still tangential) ideas. The material is inherently cumulative, though our timing for a discussion of the issues in sampling can be altered. We have found it better to cover sampling once we have introduced confidence intervals and tests so that students can appreciate the effects of sampling on these methods. The final two lectures move toward regression and can be omitted if one is pressed for time. The data in these final two lectures are, perhaps, the most interesting in the book (at least for those interested in finance).

The remainder of this preface discusses the material in the classes, with particular emphasis on the points that we try to make in each. We typically begin each class by reviewing the overview material that introduces the lecture, covering the various concepts and terminology. This "blackboard time" lays out the key ideas for the class so that students have a road map for the day. Without this introduction, we have found that some will lose sight of the concepts while focusing instead on the use of the software. Once we have the ideas down, we turn to the examples for the day, emphasizing the use of statistics to answer important business questions. Each example begins with a question, offers some relevant data, and applies statistics to answer the question.

Class 1

We use our first class as an overview and as an opportunity to set expectations. Many students have not had a good experience with statistics as undergraduates, and we find it useful to point out how this course is different from those they probably took as undergraduates. This class is also a good chance to suggest how statistics appears in their other courses, most likely finance and marketing in the MBA program.

An activity we have successfully used in this first class is an exercise in counting the number of chips in Chips Ahoy! brand chocolate chip cookies. The particular appeal of this exercise is the claim made on the package: "1,000 chips in every bag!" We have the students try to see if this claim is true. We begin by letting the students group themselves into teams of 6 to 10 members, and then give each team a sealed plastic "pouch" of cookies (about 25 cookies). Each of the packages that display the advertising claim holds two of these pouches. We leave it to the students to figure out how to verify the claim, dealing with questions such as "How many cookies should we use?" and "What's a chip?" Some have figured out that a good way to count the chips is to dissolve the cookie in water (though it can get really messy). The dough dissolves, leaving whole chips behind. Even if the students do not see to do this, the experiment works very well and makes for an intriguing, hands-on first day of class. We have also done this experiment with students working alone, but it seems to run better with teams. At the end of this exercise, we have the students report their data and we enter the data from several groups into a JMP spreadsheet with a team name and count data for, say, 10 cookies from each group. As time allows, we plot this data set to show the variation and later return to it in Class 3.

During this exercise, our focus is on variation. We want the students to recognize the presence of natural variation in the cookie-making process. This leads to some ideas from quality control. For example, it would be very expensive to have someone count out 20 chips for each cookie, and then make sure that each package had 50 cookies (for a total of exactly 1000 chips in each bag). The mass production method approximates this ideal, but in a more cost effective manner.

Class 2

This class introduces the key numerical and graphical measures of variability. As the list of topics suggests, there's a lot in this class. Students who have not seen histograms will have a hard time keeping up. However, since we do not dwell on the calculation of these summaries, but rather on their interpretation, they seem to be able to hang in there with the others. It's easy to get bogged down trying to explain the details of how to draw a boxplot, for example. We try to avoid these and keep the discussion focused on the relative merits of numerical and graphical summaries.

Some underlying themes that need to be stressed are issues of robustness (e.g., mean versus median in the presence of outliers), the use of transformations to simplify problems, and the fact that graphs are more informative than numerical summaries. Many students will not have seen a kernel density estimate, so this is a good opportunity to introduce some of the more recent developments in statistics that involve nonparametric smoothing. The availability of a slider makes this a nice showcase for what you can do with interactive software as well. Smoothing reappears in the sequel in the context of smoothing scatterplots to identify nonlinear patterns in regression analysis.

Another underlying theme of this class is the role of assumptions. For our purposes, assumptions enter indirectly (as in the choice of bin size in a histogram) or more explicitly (as in the use of the normal distribution/empirical rule). In either case, we try to comment in class on the importance of checking such assumptions via graphical diagnostics. For example, JMP's "hand tool" provides the ability to do an animated sensitivity analysis of the choices made when constructing a histogram. Though less interactive, the normal quantile plot is a graphical diagnostic for normality.

Supplemental material in this class describes graphically how one constructs a kernel density estimate since this procedure has not yet made its way into many introductory texts.

Class 3

This class has three objectives

• Use the graphical tools introduced in Class 2, giving students a second opportunity to become familiar with these techniques;

• Introduce the idea of explaining variation (albeit graphically rather than via an explicit model); and

• Do a bit of probability and quality control, which are topics covered more thoroughly in Class 4.

The quality control case is very important, and this example is the foundation for our development of standard error. The data for these shafts come from a colleague who has done considerable consulting on quality control for a major domestic auto manufacturer. We also make considerable use of plot linking in this lecture, particularly when selecting categories from histograms.

We have found that the class discussion often returns to the "cookie example" of the first day. It has an inherent grouping by the teams that collected the data. The groups may have comparable mean values, but very different variances, conveying the important message that collections of data can differ by more than their mean value (a lesson often lost by the time ANOVA comes along in subsequent courses).

Class 4

This is perhaps the most important, yet most difficult class. The difficulty arises because this class introduces standard error (SE). Standard error is hard to communicate without resorting to mathematics because it measures variation that is typically never seen, providing an estimate of the sampling variation without requiring repeated sampling.

Our method for motivating sampling variation is to use the repeated sampling associated with quality control. Rather than introduce artificially repeated samples (leading to the question "Should I take several samples?"), it makes sense in quality control that one would observe many samples. Also, the need for SE is apparent: you need SE to set limits for monitoring a process. A supplement to the first case describes why it is beneficial to look at averages rather than individual measurements.

Regarding the limits for the SD of a process, we attempt to dodge the question of how these are determined, though such questions inevitably arise in class. The JMP manual has a brief description of the procedure.

Class 5

The examples for this class are shorter than those used in the previous classes. Generally, we find that we need more "blackboard time" at this point to develop standard error. Plots such as those on the next page suggest the ideas better than more mathematics. On the left we see the population (draw something that is not normal for the population, to make the point that the CLT implies that we don't need to assume normality.) On the right, we see what happens for means of samples of 5 from this population. The means are much less variable, packed in more about μ, and their distribution is pretty close to normal. The trick, or magic, of standard error is that given one sample, we can describe how close we expect that sample mean to come to μ.

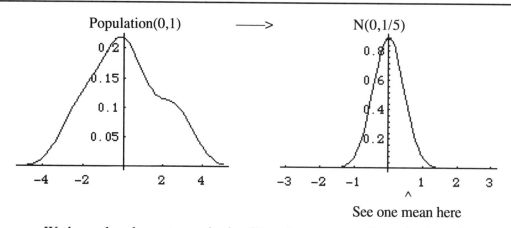

See one mean here

We have also chosen to emphasize CIs at the expense of hypothesis testing. A confidence interval is a "positive" statement about the set of plausible values for the parameter μ, whereas a test is a "negative" statement, indicating whether a value is plausible. The supplement to the first example attempts to communicate the message that tests are closely tied to confidence intervals – you reject H_0 for values outside the confidence interval. Since subsequent output will often only show the t statistic, it's good to introduce the equivalence early. We return to hypothesis tests and this correspondence in Class 7.

Class 6

One class cannot do justice to survey sampling, so we have chosen to focus on several problems that can occur. Some are obvious, such as self-selection and poor question formulation. Others are less obvious, such as the bias arising from length-biased sampling illustrated in the hotel satisfaction example of this section. We generally supplement this class with various stories from the current press. For example, students will have ample questions about polls near the time of national or important local elections. We also try to find stories from the recent press (such as clippings from the *New York Times* or *Wall Street Journal*) that illustrate the use/misuse of a survey.

This class uses two examples, one with data that you can let students find on the Internet and a second data set that we constructed to parallel a study done by a commercial hotel chain that was seriously flawed.

Class 7

This class presents two-sample comparisons, featuring both hypothesis tests and confidence intervals. In keeping with our preference for intervals over tests, we generally stick to two-sided intervals and the associated p-values. We argue that statistical tests are not terribly meaningful without a status quo that defines a null hypotheses; the examples are a bit contrived to feature such a baseline.

The first example defines the key methods. The second example, using waiting times, discusses a tempting mistake. Confidence intervals for each mean are appealing, but can be confusing when thinking about differences of means. It is tempting to work with the simpler one-sample confidence intervals and let the overlap of intervals decide comparisons. This procedure can be very conservative, and the second case shows how.

A limitation of these examples is that they only begin to address the deeper issue of decision analysis. Each decision has a cost: the cost of keeping a poor current method versus, for example, the potential gain of switching to a newer technology. Without some discussion of these issues, hypothesis testing and the associated statistics are answering the wrong question. Unfortunately, we do not have the chance to delve into more realistic decision-making which would require a more complete assessment of the costs of the alternative decisions.

The final example is supplemental; it considers the impact of non-normality upon tests and tries to implant the idea that comparisons based on means are not always the right method (in fact, they are seldom the "best" method). We generally mention the Van der Waerden method, but lack the time to discuss it more fully, appealing to the CLT. When we deliver this material at Wharton, our time in class slips from 2 hours down to 1.5 hours at this lecture. Thus, you are likely to find that you have less material for this and subsequent classes.

Class 8

Aside from the obvious paired t-test, this class introduces both dependence and correlation as well as experimental design. Dependence is the subject of Classes 10 and 11, as well as most of regression analysis. Experimental design returns in our sequel when we consider methods for the analysis of variance. Time permitting, we have on occasion done the "Coke vs. Pepsi challenge" with this lecture. It works best if you can manage to do both two-sample and paired comparisons, but that's hard to manage. The data set for the second example is constructed to resemble some marketing data received from a drug firm that was analyzing the performance of its sales field force.

Unfortunately, JMP can get in the way of the success of this class. When trying to compare a paired test to the corresponding two-sample test, the manipulations of the data (dividing the rows of a single column into several) can confuse students. If possible, have students learn how to "split" a JMP data sheet at some point prior to this class. An exercise would likely do the trick. Otherwise, the substantive content of the class (design, dependence) can be obscured by concerns over the procedural aspects of the *Tables* command.

Class 9

This class introduces the issue of confounding in a study: the groups that you want to compare are different in other aspects aside from the factor that determines group membership.

This class, with one example, provides a nice opportunity to apply some of the concepts from previous classes and review difficult ideas, such as the meaning of a p-value. The data used in this example are patterned on a large study of salary equity done at the University of Pennsylvania several years ago. Obviously, we have not used that data set, but rather constructed one with similar patterns and issues.

This data set is also used in the sequel. When we return to this problem, we show how regression analysis (rather than conditioning via subsetting) brings all of the data to bear on the question at hand, rather than just a subset.

Class 10

This class is one of the more challenging yet interesting since it mixes quite a bit of finance with the introduction of covariance. Going through this case carefully, elaborating on the needed finance, can easily consume two lecture periods. Covariance is the fundamental statistical component used in the formation of portfolios, so this example will get those who are interested in finance very engaged in the classroom discussion. Unfortunately, we also have students who, though interested in business, are not familiar with terms such as "short selling" a stock. They'll find this class more challenging since they will be trying to learn two things at once: elementary finance as well as covariance.

We have found that scatterplot matrices can consume quite a bit of classroom discussion, even though our use of them here is quite limited – we treat them as visual counterparts of a correlation matrix. It might be useful to have students work with these as part of a prior assignment so that this plot will be familiar to them.

Finally, the added note discussing the covariance of pairs of means may be of interest to those who are following the underlying details. It explains why the paired t-test works better than the two-sample t-test when the samples are correlated. The note is also important because it implies that, like data, statistics (here two sample means) can be correlated. Correlation is not just a property of data, it's also a property of the things that we compute from data. Students will need some sense of this idea to appreciate collinearity's impact on slope estimates in regression analysis.

Class 11

This class both reviews the material of the first 10 lectures as well as advertises what is to come with regression analysis. The data set is inherently interesting to explore graphically, identifying the mutual funds by name. Some of the big outliers have rather distinctive names (such as funds investing in gold) that can lead to considerable discussion in class. This case also makes a very subtle point about covariance and independence. The sample sizes for this example are quite large, some 1533 different mutual funds. These large counts lead to spuriously precise claims about the year-to-year correlation in mutual fund returns and an apparent paradox. For example, the returns in 1992 and 1993 are negatively correlated (significantly so from the regression output), whereas those for 1992 and 1991 are significantly negatively correlated.

A particularly simple explanation for this flip-flop is that the 1533 mutual funds are not independent observations. All of them invest in the same financial market and suffer common rises and falls. The 1533 funds are "worth" quite a bit fewer independent observations, to the extent that the observed changes in correlation are not surprising. Large data sets do not always imply statistical significance when correlation is present among the observations. This sort of "hidden" correlation provides fair warning to students that independence is both important and yet hard to verify. Unlike the assumption of normality or common variance across groups, there is no simple graphical tool for judging the independence of the mutual funds.

Acknowledgments

We have benefited from the help of many colleagues in preparing this material. Two have been very involved and we want to thank them here. Paul Shaman kept us honest, shared his remarkable editorial skills, and as the chairman of our department provided valuable resources. Dave Hildebrand offered numerous suggestions, and is the source of the data for many of our examples, including the car seam and computer chip data in Class 4 and the primer and food processing data in Class 7. We thank him for his generosity and encouragement along the way.

Dean P. Foster   Department of Statistics
Robert A. Stine   Wharton School
Richard P. Waterman   University of Pennsylvania
                                          Philadelphia, PA

LECTURE TEMPLATE

Quick recap of previous class

Overview and/or key application

Definitions

These won't always make sense until you have seen some data, but at least you have them written down.

Concepts

A brief overview of the new ideas we will see in each class.

Heuristics

Colloquial language, rules of thumb, etc.

Potential Confusers

Nip these in the bud.

Contents

Class 1.　Overview and Foundations

The notes for this class offer an overview of the main application areas of statistics. The key ideas to appreciate are data, variation, and uncertainty.

Topics
>　Variability
>　Randomness
>　Replication
>　Quality control

Overview of Basic Business Statistics

The essential difference between thinking about a problem from a statistical perspective as opposed to any other viewpoint is that statistics explicitly incorporates variability. What do we mean by the word "variability"? Take your admission to the MBA program as an example. Do you believe there was an element of uncertainty in it? Think about your GMAT score. If you took the test again, would you get exactly the same score? Probably not, but presumably the scores would be reasonably close. Your test score is an example of a measurement that has some variability associated with it. Now think about those phone calls to the Admissions Office. Were they always answered immediately, or did you have to wait? How long did you wait? Was it a constant time? Again, probably not. The wait time was variable. If it was too long, then maybe you just hung up and contemplated going to a different school instead. It isn't a far leap from this example to see the practical relevance of understanding variability — after all, we are talking about customer service here. How are you paying for this education? Perhaps you have invested some money; maybe you purchased some bonds. Save the collapse of the government, they are pretty certain, nonvariable, riskless investments. Perhaps, however, you have invested in the stock market. This certainly is riskier than buying bonds. Do you know how much your return on these stocks will be in two years? No, since the returns on the stock market are variable. What about car insurance? If you have registered your car in Philadelphia then you have seen the insurance market at work. Why is the insurance so high? Most likely the high rates are the result of large numbers of thefts and uninsured drivers. Is your car certain to be stolen? Of course not, but it might be. The status of your car in two years, either stolen or not stolen, is yet another "variable" displaying uncertainty and variation.

The strength of statistics is that it provides a means and a method for extracting, quantifying, and understanding the nature of the variation in each of these questions. Whether the underlying issue is car insurance, investment strategies, computer network traffic, or educational testing, statistics is the way to describe the variation concisely and provide an angle from which to base a solution.

What This Material Covers

A central theme of these case studies is variability, its measurement and exploitation in decision-making situations. A dual theme is that of modeling. In statistics, modeling can be described as the process by which one explains variability.

For an example, let's go back to the question about car insurance. Why are the rates high? We have already said that it's probably because there are many thefts and lots of uninsured drivers. But your individual insurance premium depends on many other factors as well, some of which you can control while others are outside your reach. Your age is extremely important, as is your prior driving history. The number of years you have had your license is yet another factor in the equation that makes up your individual insurance premium. International students face real challenges! These factors, or variables as we are more likely to call them, are ways of explaining the variability in individual insurance rates. Putting the factors together in an attempt to explain insurance premiums is an example of "building a model." The model-building process — how to do it and how to critique it — is the main topic of this text. In this course, you will learn about variability. In our sequel, *Business Analysis Using Regression* you can learn about using models to explain variability.

What Is Not Covered Here

A common misconception about statistics is that it is an endless list of formulas to be memorized and applied. This is not our approach. We are more concerned about understanding the ideas on a conceptual level and leveraging the computational facilities available to us as much as possible. Virtually no formulas and very little math appears. Surprisingly, rather than making our job easier, it actually makes it far more of a challenge. No more hiding behind endless calculations; they will happen in a nanosecond on the computer. We will be involved in the more challenging but rewarding work of understanding and interpreting the results and trying to do something useful with them!

Key Application

Quality control. In any manufacturing or service-sector process, variability is most often an undesirable property. Take grass seed, for example. Many seed packets display the claim "only 0.4% weed seed." The manufacturer has made a statement; for the consumer to retain confidence in the manufacturer, the statement should be at least approximately true. Ensuring that the weed content is only 0.4% is a quality control problem. No one believes that it will be exactly 0.4000000% in every packet, but it better be close. Perhaps 0.41% or 0.39% is acceptable. Setting these limits and ensuring adherence to them is what quality control is all about. We accept that there is some variability in the weed content, so we want to measure it and use our knowledge of the variability to get an idea of how frequently the quality limits will be broken.

Quality applies equally well to service-sector processes. How long you wait for the telephone to be answered by the admissions office is such a process. The variability of wait times needs to be measured and controlled in order to avoid causing problems to people that must wait inordinate amounts of time.

Definitions

Variability, variation. These represent the degree of change from one item to the next, as in the variability in the heights, weights, or test scores of students in a statistics class. The larger the variation, the more spread out the measurements tend to be. If the heights of all the students were constant, there would be no variability in heights.

Randomness. An event is called "random", or said to display "randomness," if its outcome is uncertain before it happens. Examples of random events include
  • the value of the S&P500 index tomorrow afternoon (assuming it's a weekday!),
  • whether or not a particular consumer purchases orange juice tomorrow,
  • the number of O-rings that fail during the next space shuttle launch.

Replication. Recognizing that variability is an important property, we clearly need to measure it. For a variability measure to be accurate or meaningful, we need to repeat samples taken under similar conditions. Otherwise we are potentially comparing apples with oranges. This repetition is called "replication." In practice it is often not clear that the conditions are similar, and so this similarity becomes an implicit assumption in a statistical analysis.

Heuristics

Heuristics are simple descriptions of statistical concepts put into everyday language. As such, they are not exact statements or even necessarily technically correct. Rather, they are meant to provide an illuminating and alternative viewpoint.

Variability. One way of thinking about variability is as the antithesis of information. You can think about an inverse relationship between variability and information. The more variability in a process the less information you have about that process. Obtaining a lot of information is synonymous with having low variability.

Information is also close to the concept of precision. The more information you have, the more precise a statement you can make. Engineers love precision; components manufactured with high precision have low variability. So an alternative way of thinking about variability is by considering the way it is inversely related to information and precision. That is, as variability increases, information and precision decrease. Conversely, as variability decreases, information and precision increase.

Potential Confusers

What's the difference between a "variable" and "variability"?

A variable is a measurement or value that displays variability across the sampled items. For example, the number of chocolate chips in a cookie is a variable, and the range in counts seen for different cookies is a measure of the variability.

Class 2. Statistical Summaries of Data

This class introduces simple, effective ways of describing data. All of the computations and graphing will be done by JMP. Our task — and it is the important task — is to learn how to selectively interpret the results and communicate them to others. The priorities are as follows: first, displaying data in useful, clear ways; second, interpreting summary numbers sensibly.

The examples of this class illustrate that data from diverse applications often share characteristic features, such as a bell-shaped (or normal) histogram. When data have this characteristic, we can relate various summary measures to the concentration of the data, arriving at the so-called empirical rule. The empirical rule is our first example of a useful consequence of a statistical model, in this case the normal model for random data. Whenever we rely upon a model such as this, we need to consider diagnostics that can tell us how well our model matches the observed data. Most of the diagnostics, like the normal quantile plot introduced in this lecture, are graphical.

Topics

    Pictures: Histograms, boxplots, and smooth density plots

                 Diagnostic plot for the normal model (normal quantile plot)

                 Time series plots

    Summaries: Measures of location: sample mean, median

                 Measures of scale: standard deviation, interquartile range, variance

    Concepts: Normal distribution

                 Empirical rule

                 Skewness and outliers

Examples

    GMAT scores

        Fundamental numerical and graphical summaries, smoothing

    Returns on General Motors stock

        Time series, trends, and the transformation to percentage change

    Skewness in executive compensation

        All data are not normal, but transformations can remedy some of the

        deviations from normality

Key Applications

The 10 minute summary. Put yourself in the following scenario: you work for a company that sells compact discs (of the musical type) over the Internet. You obtain the ages of potential customers by having people who hit your home page fill in an on-line form. Of course, the age distribution of your customers may affect the sort of material you should stock. The good news is that all the age data take a single column of a spreadsheet. The bad news is that the spreadsheet generated from last week's hits has 4231 rows, and you have just ten minutes to summarize the customer age profile before a critical meeting.

Poring over all 4231 rows is a brain-numbing and time-consuming task. Fortunately, through the use of a small number of well-chosen statistical graphics accompanied by several statistical summary measures, it is possible to make the required summary very quickly. This potential for a fast and efficient summary of large amounts of data is one of the strongest reasons for doing a statistical analysis.

Daily earnings at risk. Keeping senior management informed of the risks of trading and investment operations of a financial institution is paramount. An important piece of information is known as the "daily earnings at risk, " an estimate of the maximum losses on a given position that can be expected over 24 hours with 95% probability. In this class we will see what is involved in such a calculation, focusing on the statistical aspects of the problem. The two key pieces of statistical knowledge are

1. that daily returns approximately follow a normal distribution and

2. the *empirical rule*, which provides a way of estimating probabilities for normal distributions.

Definitions

Sample mean. This is the average value of a set of measurements, computed as the sum of all the measurements divided by the number of measurements (typically labeled n). Visually, the sample mean is the balancing point of the histogram.

Sample median. The observation that falls in the middle when the data are put into order. The median is also known as the "50th percentile."

Sample variance. The average squared distance in a sample of an observation to the sample mean.

Sample standard deviation (SD). The square root of the sample variance, and thus measured in the same units as the initial data. The variance, on the other hand, is measured on the scale of "squared units."

Sample interquartile range (IQR). The distance between the 25th percentile and the 75th percentile.

Skewness. The absence of symmetry in the histogram of a collection of data.

Outlier. An atypical observation that is separated from the main cluster of the data. Outliers are important in statistical analyses. Such observations have a dramatic effect on summary statistics such as the sample mean and the sample standard deviation. Often, if we can learn what makes the outlier unusual, we may discover that an important factor has been left out of our analysis.

Concepts

Normal distribution. In many areas it's fair to say that 5% of the tools do 95% of the work. Some tools are extremely useful, relevant, and accurate. In statistics the normal distribution (or normal curve) is such a tool. Understanding it well now will carry over to future classes.

The normal distribution, or "bell curve" as it is sometimes colloquially referred to, is often able to summarize data adequately for many practical and diverse applications, ranging from daily returns on equities to variability in the heights of human beings to the logarithm of family incomes in the United States. The idea is simple: draw a histogram of your data and join the tops of the bars. The resulting curve is often well approximated by a normal distribution.

Although there are an infinite number of possible normal distributions, it takes only two numbers to identify any particular one. These numbers are the mean and the standard deviation of the data. This implies that if you believe your data follow a normal distribution, you don't need to carry all that data around. The person who knows only the mean and the standard deviation knows just as much about the data as the person who has all the raw data. For example, in the first key application listed above, it may be possible to use the mean and standard deviation to summarize the ages of all the people who hit the home page.

The empirical rule. The empirical rule pulls together the two summaries (mean and standard deviation) for a normal distribution into one of the most simple but powerful ideas in statistics: that 95% of your data will lie within ±2 SD of the mean, and conversely only 5% will lie outside this range.

Diagnostic. A method (often graphical) for assessing the credibility of an assumption. Because the normal distribution is so important and convenient, we need to have some methods at hand to assess the viability of such an assumption. One of the emphases in this course will be "diagnostics." We will encounter them in many different contexts. Checking assumptions through diagnostics is one of the ways to evaluate the worth of someone else's work, so you can think of diagnostics as "evaluation tools."

Heuristics

If data have an approximately symmetric, bell-shaped distribution, then 95% of the data lie within ±2 SD of the mean, also known as the empirical rule.

Potential Confusers

Population parameters and sample statistics. A population parameter is an attribute associated with an entire population. For example, the current population of the United States has a mean age. Every population parameter can be estimated by a sample statistic. The population mean can be estimated by the sample mean, the population variance by the sample variance, and so on. More often than not, the population parameter is unknown. That is why we try to estimate it through a sample statistic: if we knew the population parameters, there would be no need to estimate them with statistics!

Why have both measures, the sample variance and the sample standard deviation? The important aspect of the sample standard deviation is that it is measured on the same scale as the data. For instance, if the raw data is measured in dollars then so is its standard deviation, but the sample variance would be measured in dollars^2. The variance, on the other hand, is useful for doing certain calculations such as those used to estimate the risk of a stock portfolio (see Class 10). In general, the SD is more useful for interpretation; the variance is more handy for math calculations.

Why is there that n-1 divisor in the book's formula for the sample variance? It's done for technical reasons having to do with the fact that we'd really like to know the variation about the population mean μ rather than the sample average. Fortunately, the difference is not important for moderately large sample sizes.

GMAT Scores

GMAT.jmp

What is the typical GMAT score for students who come to Wharton? Are all of the scores very close to each other?

This data set consists of GMAT test scores submitted by 724 members of the Wharton Class of 1994. As a first step to this (and any) analysis, spend a few moments browsing through the data shown in the opening spreadsheet view. Having done this, we begin our analysis with a graphical summary of the data, using the *Distribution of Y* command from the *Analyze* menu of JMP.

The initial display shows a histogram with a boxplot. The accompanying "boxplot" highlights the middle 50% of the data and identifies several outliers with relatively low scores. The data are slightly skewed toward smaller scores; after all, you cannot score above 800 (though some students came quite close!). The brackets outside the boxplot show the range spanned by the "shortest half" of the data — that collection of 50% of the observations which are most tightly packed together. For data that are symmetric and unimodal (one area of concentration in the histogram), the box and the bracket agree.

GMAT

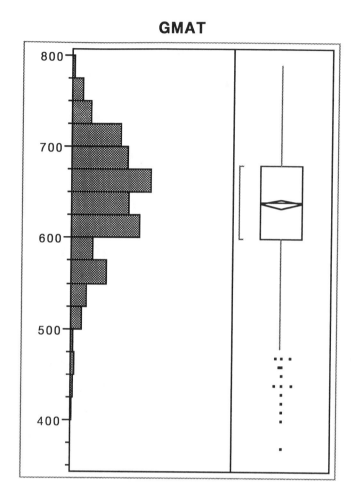

We can obtain other plots by modifying this summary using the options revealed by the check-marked button at the bottom of the JMP display. (The $ button lets you save things, and the * button lets you annotate saved summaries, which are called journal entries in JMP parlance.) When several outliers occur near the same value, JMP plots them side-by-side, as seen here, to avoid over-printing (and thus hiding) the multiple values.

The boxplot is very concise and is most useful when comparing batches of numbers. Class 3 includes an example of the use of boxplots for comparing sets of numbers. For now, make sure you can relate the appearance of the boxplot to the histogram and know what the lines in the boxplot represent.

Here are the associated summary statistics reported with the histogram summary. The quantiles are also known as percentiles. The mean and median are estimates of location for the data, whereas the median, interquartile range (IQR) and range are measures of variation or spread. Our concern is not the calculation of these; any computer can do that. Instead, our focus is on how to use these summaries and to be aware of features in the data that make these measures misleading.

Quantiles

maximum	100.0%	790.00	
	99.5%	780.00	
	97.5%	750.00	
	90.0%	720.00	
quartile	75.0%	680.00	
median	50.0%	640.00	centerline of boxplot
quartile	25.0%	600.00	
	10.0%	550.00	
	2.5%	490.00	
	0.5%	416.25	
minimum	0.0%	370.00	

Moments

Mean	638.6326
Std Dev	65.9660
...	
N	724.

The quantiles (or percentiles) determine the appearance of the boxplot, as the following illustration shows. The length of the boxplot is the distance between the upper and lower quartile, known as the interquartile range (IQR). We will explain the diamond in the middle of the boxplot later in Class 5 when we discuss confidence intervals.

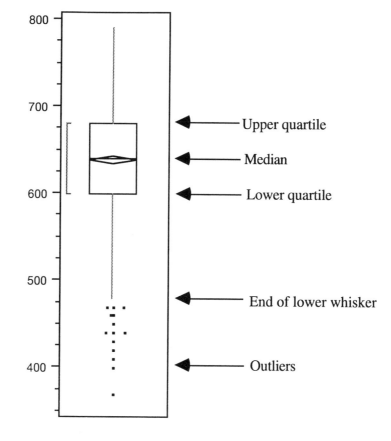

The histogram offers a rather lumpy image of the variation among the 724 GMAT scores. The histogram image depends on where we locate the bins and the width of the bins. Experimenting with the *Hand* cursor lets you resize the histogram bins. Moving the hand cursor to the left or right decreases or increases the number of bins used in the histogram. Moving the cursor up or down shifts the origin of the bins.

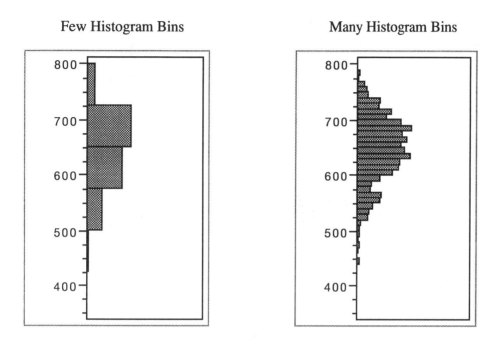

A question to resolve is "What is the right bin size?" Using a very wide bin size as on the left makes the skewness in the scores evident, but conceals other features of the data. Using a very narrow size suggests that the data are bimodal, perhaps consisting of two groups of observations. But is the small peak on the low side of the scale meaningful, or is it merely the byproduct of random variation and "data mining"? Statistical results often depend on certain assumptions that dictate how the analysis is to be done. In this case the choice of the bin width is crucial. *One should always assess the sensitivity to important assumptions and choices.* The interactive use of the hand tool makes it simple for us to judge how the bin size affects the appearance of the histogram.

Modern renderings of the distribution of a single batch of data avoid the question of where to locate the bins and focus on how "smooth" the estimated density estimate should be. For this series of plots, the horizontal layout option fits four plots on a page. The *Kernel Std* parameter controls the smoothness of the superimposed curves. Which is right? Is the bump real? It's hard to say.

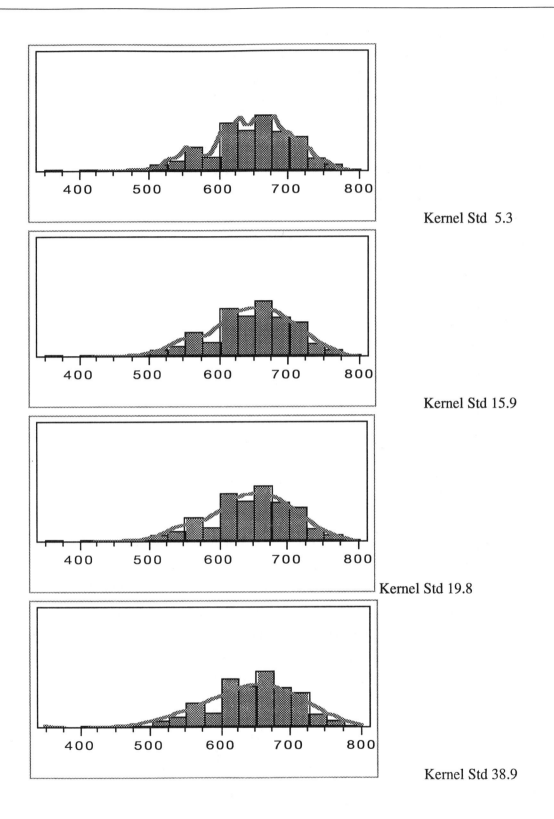

Kernel Std 5.3

Kernel Std 15.9

Kernel Std 19.8

Kernel Std 38.9

The shape of the last smooth kernel density estimate suggests a popular model for characterizing random variation — that provided by the normal distribution. The normal curve (shown in red on the screen or the heavy line below) superimposed over the histogram in the next plot is identified by only two summary measures from the data: the sample mean and the sample standard deviation. The normal curve will always be symmetric and bell-shaped, regardless of the shape of the histogram.

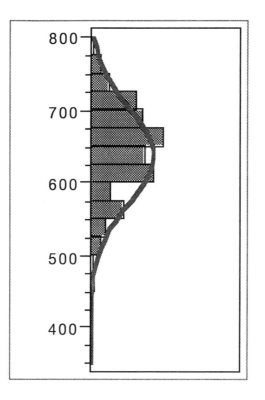

Here is a comparison to the smooth density estimate that does not make the assumption of a normal distribution. The normal curve is red on the screen and appears here as the darker of the two superimposed curves. Again, the choice of which is best depends on how smooth we are willing to require our estimated curve to be.

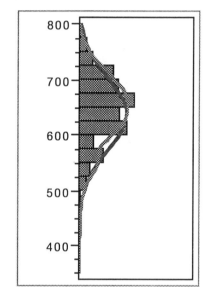

If we decide the normal model is a reasonable characterization of the variation among GMAT scores, we can reduce our analysis of this data to two summary measures: the sample mean (or average) and the sample standard deviation. Under the normal model, the rest of the information in the 724 scores is uninformative random variation.

The so-called empirical rule for data that have a normal (or bell-shaped) histogram indicates that about 2/3 of the observations in the population lie within a standard deviation of the mean, and about 95% lie within 2 standard deviations. The usual notation for a normal population, to distinguish it from a sample of data, denotes the mean or center of the population by μ and its standard deviation by σ. These two values determine the concentration of the data at the center.

The following small table shows how the mean μ and standard deviation σ of the population determine the concentration of the data.

Interval	Proportion of Data
$[\mu - \sigma, \ \mu + \sigma]$	68.27%, about $2/3$
$[\mu - 2\sigma, \mu + 2\sigma]$	95.44%, about $19/20$
$[\mu - 3\sigma, \mu + 3\sigma]$	99.73%, just about everything

These simple rules and the symmetry of the normal curve allow you to answer some interesting questions. For example, based on only the mean and the standard deviation, what proportion of scores would you expect to exceed 705? Replacing the unknown population values μ and σ by the sample values $\overline{X}$ and SD, we see that

score above 705 $\iff$ score 1 SD above the mean $\iff$ $(706–639)/66 \approx 1$

Thus, we would expect only about $1/2 \times 1/3 = 1/6 \approx 0.17$ above this value. Checking the data (which we know are not exactly normally distributed), we see that the fraction larger than 705 is

$$\frac{724\text{-}615}{724} = \frac{109}{724} = .15 \ .$$

Pretty close. Although we know that the normal model is not perfect for these data, we can still use it and the empirical rule to approximate how the data vary. For example, the empirical rule suggests that the interval

$$[\text{mean} \pm 2 \ \text{SD}] = [639 - 2 \times 66, 639 + 2 \times 66] = [507, 771]$$

ought to hold about 95% of the data. In fact, 96.4% of the scores (698 of the 724) fall into this range. The empirical rule is close even though the data are skewed.empirical rule

The normal model is so common and important that we need some *diagnostics* to judge how appropriate it is for a given problem. Graphical diagnostics are the best. Histograms offer a start in this direction, but we need something better. Deviations from normality most often appear in the extremes of the data, and these are hard to judge from the histogram since the height of the histogram is so small in this area.

In contrast, the normal quantile plot (obtained via the check button when viewing a histogram) shows the closeness to normality throughout the range of the data, with a particular emphasis in the extremes of the distribution.

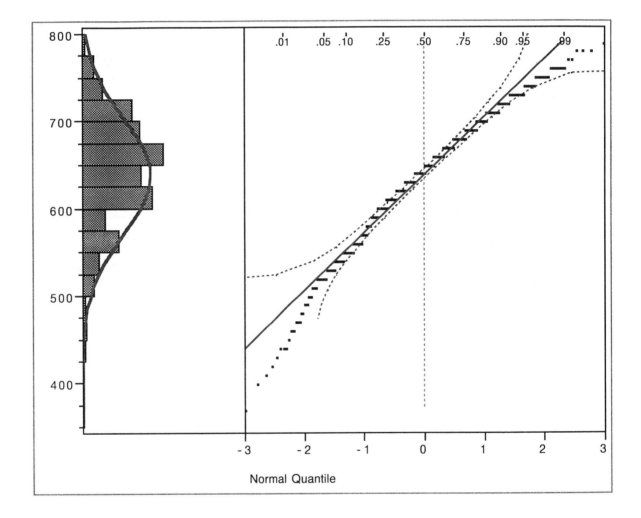

In the normal quantile plot, the shown data points fall along the diagonal line (shown in red on the computer screen) if the data fit the normal model. The dashed bands around this diagonal line indicate where, if ever, the histogram deviates from normality. The magnifying lens tool in JMP is useful here to get a better look at whether the points go outside these bands. In this figure the points deviate from the line and suggest that the data are not normal. Indeed, a test for normality finds convincing evidence that the normal model is not correct here — nonetheless, it is not a bad first-order approximation, or "working model."

This plot is constructed using the same calculations that we used to check the empirical rule with this data. The value 1 on the lower horizontal axis labeled "Normal Quantile" corresponds to the value $\overline{X}$ + SD, 1 standard deviation above the sample mean. Under normality, about 83% of the data should be less than this value. The idealized percentages are shown along the upper horizontal axis at the top of the figure. The height of the diagonal reference line is determined by applying the empirical rule. Based on the empirical rule and the sample average and SD, the value corresponding to 1 SD above the mean is $639 + 66 = 705$. Similarly, the value at 0 SDs above the mean is just the sample average, 639. The plot is scaled so that these values implied by the empirical rule fall on a line, which becomes the reference line in the figure.

What is the typical GMAT score for students who come to Wharton? Are all of the scores very close to each other?

The average GMAT for this class is 639, but there is also quite a bit of variation about the mean. The normal model provides a good approximation to the distribution of the scores, allowing us to summarize the distribution of scores via its mean and standard deviation.

The various plots of the distribution of the data suggest some moderate skewness, with the distribution skewed toward smaller values.

Some Notes on the Kernel Density Estimate.

A kernel density estimate is constructed by adding together small "bumps" known as kernels to form a smooth density estimate (as opposed to the ragged, rectangular shape of the histogram). The idea is to place a smooth curve at the location of each observation on the x-axis. These are shown in gray below for a small data set of six observations, {0, 3, 5, 6, 7, 9}, highlighted by dots in the figure. The heights of the gray curves, the kernels, are added together to yield the final kernel density estimate, which is shown in black. Since the area under each of the kernels is $1/n = 1/6$, the area under the final density estimate is one.

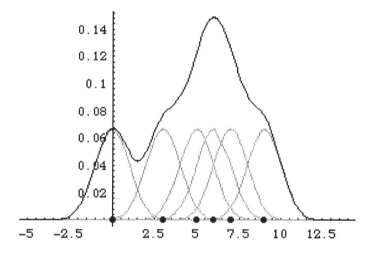

As you vary the slider provided by JMP, you change the width of these underlying kernels. For the example shown above, the width setting is 1. Moving the width up to 2 gives wider kernels, and a smoother density estimate which obliterates the mode on the left that came from the point at zero which is separated from the rest of the data.

The figure shown below shows the new kernel density, with the width set to 2. The larger width blurs the distinction of the point at 0 from the others, leading to a smoother density estimate.

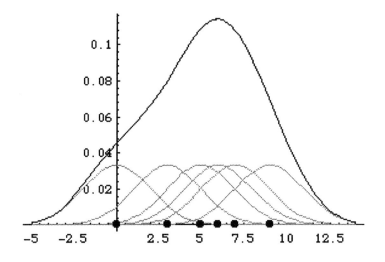

Returns on General Motors Stock

GM92.jmp and GM87.jmp

What is the typical return on GM common stock? Since the value of GM stock varies from day to day, how much might the price swing from one day to the next? Does the rate of return compensate for the uncertainty or "risk" in owning GM stock?

This analysis considers the daily price of General Motors common stock over several years. We begin the analysis by looking at plots of the price of the stock over the two years 1992 and 1993. Taking the approach of many financial analysts, we then convert the data into relative changes, looking at the ratio

$$\text{RelChange} = \frac{\text{Price today} - \text{Price yesterday}}{\text{Price yesterday}}$$

as a measure of the return on the stock. This simple transformation has a remarkable effect on our analysis. The histogram of GM stock returns during these years deviates from the normal model, particularly in the extremes of the data. The deviations from normality are more evident in the normal quantile plot at the right than in the histogram with the superimposed normal curve on the left.

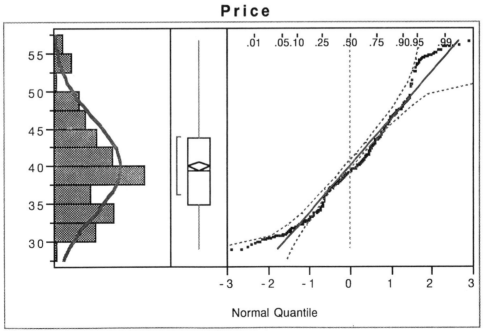

Does the histogram conceal important characteristics of the GM prices? Whenever data are measured over time, forming a time series, it is important to plot them sequentially as done below. Omitting such a time series plot hides the dependence in the data over time. One should never examine the histogram of a time series without checking first for the presence of trend.

A time series plot of the stock prices shows an overall impressive upward trend, along with what for investors are some unsettling periods of declining price. The price of the stock roughly doubled over the two years 1992 and 1993 in spite of the periods of decline. (This point plot is obtained via the *Fit Y by X* command of the *Analyze* menu; use the *Overlay* command of the *Graphics* menu for connected line plots.)

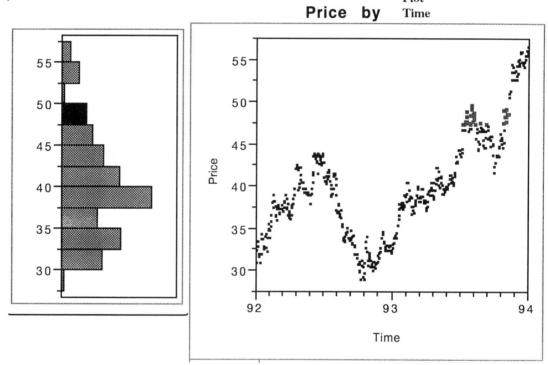

Notice the highlighting in this aligned pair of plots. By clicking with the mouse on the bin just below 50 in the histogram, we see these same points highlighted in the sequence plot on the right. This is an example of plot linking: points highlighted in one display are similarly shown in other views. The histogram does not indicate that the prices in this bin occur in two very different periods, one at a peak and one during a rise in price. The histogram can be very misleading when used to summarize a time series that shows regular trends.

The variation in the price of this stock translates into "risk." Intuitively, a stock is a risky asset since its value changes in an unpredictable manner. Unlike a bank account with a guaranteed rate of interest and growth over time, the value of most stocks moves up and down. In this case, had you owned GM stock near the end of 1992 and needed to sell shares to raise cash, it would have been unfortunate since the value was so low at that time.

The following plot (generated using the *Overlay Plots* platform of the JMP *Graph* menu) contrasts the irregular price of GM's stock — the risky asset — with the constant growth of a risk-free asset growing at a steady annual rate of 5%. The asset and the stock are both worth $31 at the start of 1992. In this example, the stock wins big over the long haul, falling behind only near the end of 1992. We will return to further comparisons of these types of assets in Class 11.

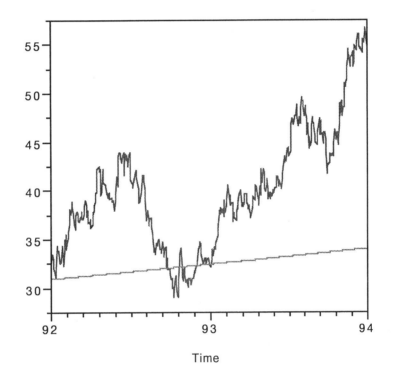

Time

We can enhance the trend in the price data by smoothing out the irregular random variation via a smoothing spline. Use the fitting button on the screen under the scatterplot to add this trend to the plot. In this case we have used the "flexible" version with parameter lambda = 0.01, a somewhat subjective choice.

Price by Time (with smooth)

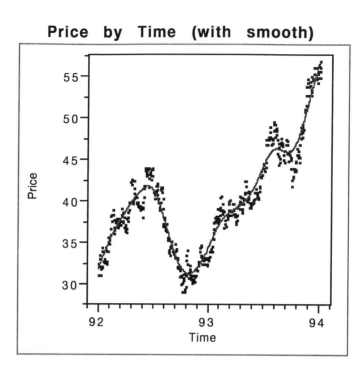

The relative changes, in contrast to the actual prices, show a very irregular, random pattern. Again, the relative changes are defined as the change from one day to the next divided by the price on the previous day,

$$\text{RelChange} = \frac{\text{Price today} - \text{Price yesterday}}{\text{Price yesterday}} .$$

The horizontal line in the sequence plot is the average return over this period, obtained by using the *Fitting* button to add the mean to the plot. It is ever so slightly positive. In the absence of trend, the histogram is once again a useful summary of the distribution of the data.

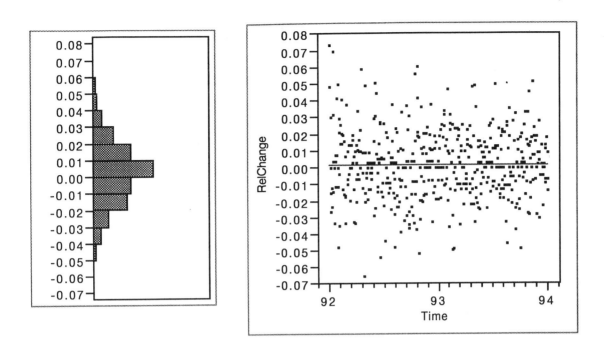

The flexible smooth curve shows no evidence of trend either, just small oscillations about the mean.

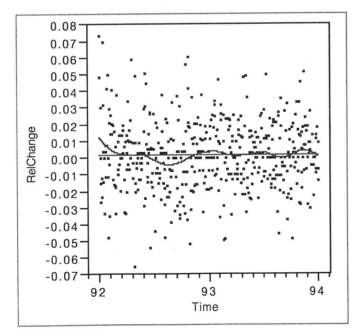

Here is a more complete summary of the relative changes. As with the GMAT scores, the normal model is a good working model or working approximation. (The flat spot in the middle of the quantile plot shows a collection of zeros in the data — days on which the value of the stock did not change.) In contrast, the daily relative change of the risk-free asset is only 0.000188 (giving the 5% annual rate of growth), compared to 0.0016 for the stock. By comparison, there is no variance in the growth of the risk-free asset.

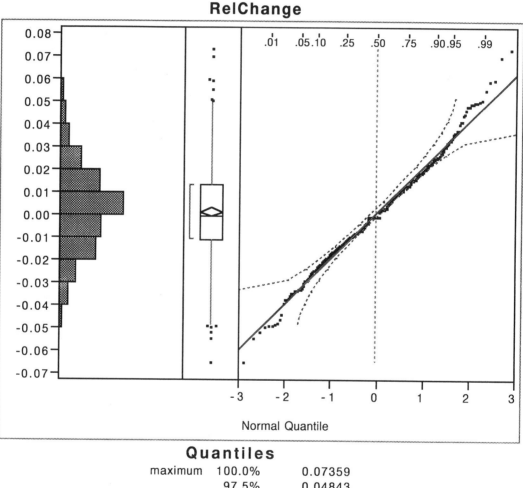

RelChange

Quantiles

maximum	100.0%	0.07359
	97.5%	0.04843
quartile	75.0%	0.01357
median	50.0%	0.00000
quartile	25.0%	-0.011
	2.5%	-0.0369
minimum	0.0%	-0.0649

Moments

Mean	0.0016
Std Dev	0.0202
...	
N	507.

Our analysis now changes to the two years 1987 and 1988. The prices of GM stock during these two years show the effects of the stock market fall of October 1987. The decrease in value was rather sudden and interrupted a pattern of generally increasing prices. The plot also shows the comparable risk-free asset (the steadily growing line), again growing at a steady 5% rate from the same initial value as the stock. In contrast to the two-year period 1992 and 1993, the slow but steady rate of growth has some real appeal here, even though at the end of two years the value of the risk-free asset is much smaller.

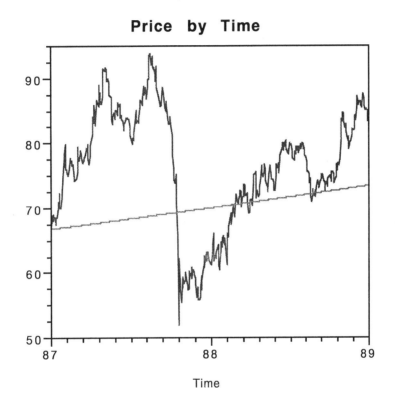

Price by Time

The sudden fall in price generates outliers in the relative changes (in rows 202 and 203, corresponding to October 19 and 20, 1987). Two outliers dominate the plot. Unless we set these two very large outliers aside, they will dominate most plots of this data. Most of the data are compressed into a small portion of the display, with the outliers along the fringe. As before, the horizontal line is the average daily return, which is slightly positive.

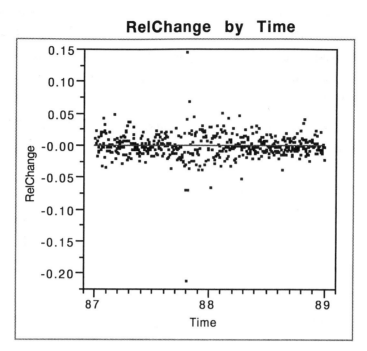

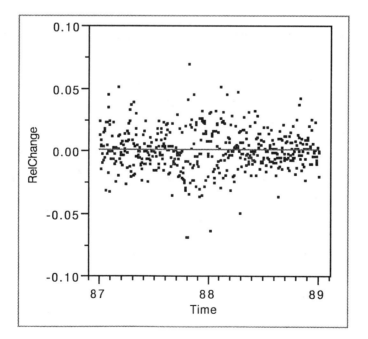

One way to handle the compression effect caused by the outliers is to rescale the vertical axis of this plot, and zoom in on the center of the data. A double-click on the vertical axis of the figure opens a dialog box that allows us to change the range of values shown in the figure (in this case, from -0.10 to 0.10).

Hiding observations by rescaling the plot works well but quickly becomes tiresome as one views more and more plots. It is easy, however, to exclude these outlying values from our analysis. By doing so, we are able to see whatever pattern there might be in the remaining data that would otherwise be too compressed to appreciate without having to continually rescale the figures.

To set the outliers aside, select the points using the cursor tool (holding down the Shift key lets us select several at once) and then, from the *Rows* menu, choose the *Exclude* command. (Note how the excluded observations are marked in the row label area of the spreadsheet.)

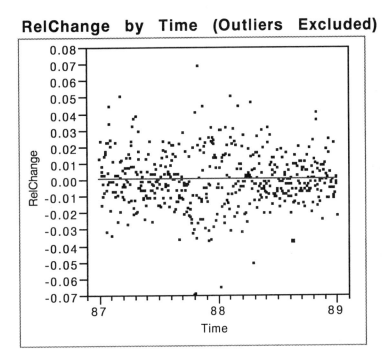

A closer look at the variation in the data (excluding the outliers from October 19 and 20) shows that other outliers lie on the fringe of this data set as well. In the center of the data, though, the normal quantile plot shows that the distribution of the returns is clearly rather normal. Once again, the normal model is a good working approximation, allowing us to compress these 504 values into two summary measures, the mean and the standard deviation.

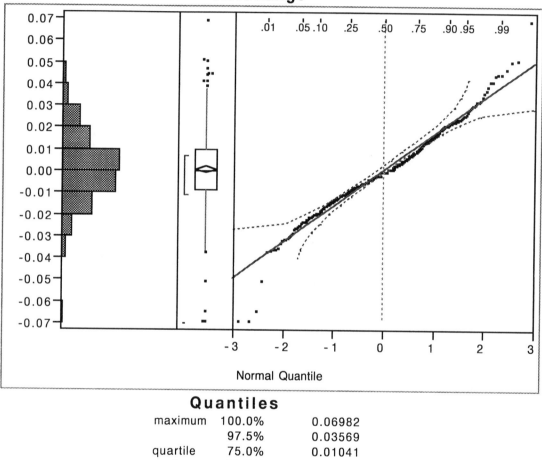

RelChange

Quantiles

maximum	100.0%	0.06982
	97.5%	0.03569
quartile	75.0%	0.01041
median	50.0%	0.00000
quartile	25.0%	-0.0084
	2.5%	-0.0311
minimum	0.0%	-0.0688

Moments

Mean		0.0011
Std Dev		0.0166
...		
N		504.

What is the typical return on GM common stock? Since the value of GM stock varies from day to day, how much might the price swing from one day to the next? Does the rate of return compensate for the uncertainty or "risk" in owning GM stock?

The average return in both periods is slightly positive, consistent with the generally upward trend in the prices. But is this reward worth the risk associated with the swings in price? That would depend on where else you could invest the money, and the associated rate of return for a risk free asset such as a treasury bond.

How would you feel about owning an investment that performs well on most days, but occasionally decreases in value? We will return to this question later when we look at portfolios in Class 10.

A Note on Relative Changes

Before concluding, we want to mention a different transformation that is sometimes used in financial analyses. An alternative to percentage change which frequently appears is the log (natural log) of the ratio of today's price to yesterday's price,

$$\text{LogRelative} = \log_e \frac{\text{Price today}}{\text{Price yesterday}} \ .$$

For processes with small changes, both transformations give comparable results. To convince yourself (without getting into the details), compare RelChange to LogRelative when the prices are 100 and 101:

$$\text{RelChange} = \frac{101\text{-}100}{100} = 0.01 \qquad \text{LogRelative} = \log_e \frac{101}{100} = 0.00995 \approx 0.01$$

Skewness in Executive Compensation

Forbes94.jmp

What is the distribution of executive compensation for 790 executives as reported by *Forbes*? Are these executives overpaid?

Not all data are normally distributed. Although both the Wharton GMAT scores and the relative changes of GM stock look fairly normal, do not get the impression that all data are normally distributed with just an outlier here and there. Often, the deviation from normality is considerable and not the result of the presence of a few rogue values.

Common situations leading to data that are not normal are those that have a natural attainable limit (typically zero). For example, data that count the number of occurrences of events or data that measure of the length of time required to accomplish some task will not be normally distributed. Rather, values will often accumulate near zero and gradually decay. Income data are another popular example of data that are not normally distributed. Both of these distributions are said to be right skewed.

The data for this example are taken from the May 23, 1994 issue of *Forbes*. Each year around this time, Forbes publishes an article that deals with the pay of top corporate executives. The data in this issue is more extensive than what we have used here, so you might want to take a look at his issue (Volume 153, n.11, pages 144-198) or one of the more recent studies.

The distribution of incomes of executives from the *Forbes* survey is so skewed that the default histogram has but a single bin. Who made $200,000,000 for the year? Using the names of the executives as point labels, we can see that it's Michael Eisner of Disney. The *Financial Times* reports (2/24/97) that he is jockeying for a similar compensation package in 1997, one so large that some large shareholders are getting angry.

Because of the outlier, the mean compensation (about $2.8 million) is larger than the upper quartile ($2.5 million). With the outlier, the average compensation is larger than more than 75% of the executive compensations. By comparison, the median compensation is $1.3 million and much more descriptive of the typical executive compensation. For data that are heavily skewed with extreme outliers, the sample mean is usually not very representative.

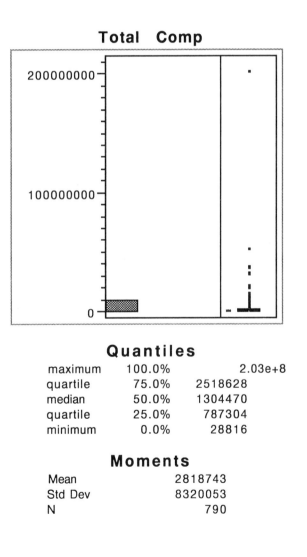

Total Comp

Quantiles

maximum	100.0%	2.03e+8
quartile	75.0%	2518628
median	50.0%	1304470
quartile	25.0%	787304
minimum	0.0%	28816

Moments

Mean	2818743
Std Dev	8320053
N	790

Setting one or even several outliers aside is seldom a cure for skewness. With one outlier (Eisner of Disney) set aside, we get the following summary. In a crude sense, this one outlier "explains" much of the variation in the original data. The SD with Eisner is $8.3 million; without Eisner, the SD drops down to $4.3 million, about half of its original value. In terms of variances (which square the SDs) this one outlier — one point out of 790 — accounts for about $3/4$ of the variation in the original data.

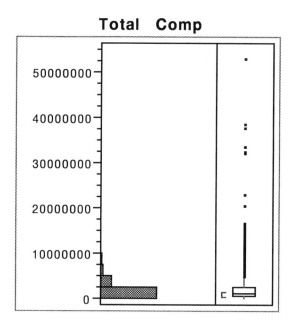

Total   Comp

Moments

Mean	2565003
Std Dev	4287543
N	789

With eight more outliers removed, the distribution of these data remains heavily skewed. We can see more structure, but most of the data remains compressed at the bottom of the display. The skewness is not so severe, but how long should we consider removing observations? Each time we remove the most extreme, others take that place.

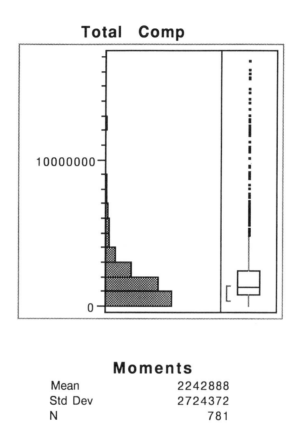

Total Comp

Moments

Mean	2242888
Std Dev	2724372
N	781

Transformations offer an alternative approach that lets us use *all* of the data at once, if we can learn to live with and interpret the new data. A nonlinear transformation such as a logarithm is able to reveal more of the differences among the observations that make up samples which are skewed like this compensation data. Taking logs to the base 10 groups the incomes by the number of digits in total compensation. Most of the executives have at least a six-figure income. The logged data are almost normal — without setting observations aside. Some outliers and skewness persist, but we get a more revealing picture that spreads the data more evenly along the axis of the histogram rather than leaving them compressed in one or two cells.

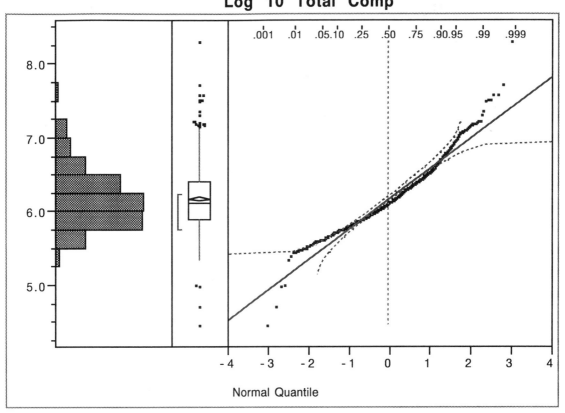

On this transformed scale, the mean and median are rather close together.

Quantiles

maximum	100.0%	8.3075
quartile	75.0%	6.4012
median	50.0%	6.1154
quartile	25.0%	5.8961
minimum	0.0%	4.4596

Moments

Mean	6.1778
Std Dev	0.4121
N	790

What is the distribution of executive compensation for 790 executives as reported by *Forbes*? Are these executives overpaid?

The compensation data are heavily skewed, but are the executives overpaid? Current press reports suggest that stock holders think that some of them are, especially given the growth of these incomes (up 12% from the previous year). To determine if the executes are overpaid, one would need to consider the performance of the companies that they manage, and perhaps compare them to peers in comparable situations.

This example illustrates the sensitivity to outliers of numerical summaries, particularly the mean and the SD. The mean compensation dropped by 9% (from $2.819 million to $2.565 million) when one observation, Eisner of Disney, was excluded from the analysis. A single observation (less than 0.13% of the data) has a huge effect on the average compensation. The standard deviation is even more affected. With Eisner, the SD is $8.3 million. Without Eisner, it is almost half this size, dropping to $4.3 million. Rank-based statistics such as the median and the interquartile range (IQR, the length of the box in the boxplot) are much less affected by wild, outlying values. In this example, both are essentially unchanged when Eisner is removed from the data. Even when we remove eight more of the outliers, the median and IQR are virtually unchanged.

Finally, and perhaps most importantly, we need to give some thought to the relevance and interpretation of data on a log scale. Sure, the histogram of the transformed data looks more like that of a normal sample, but no one I know is paid in "log dollars." The value of logarithms for interpretation has to do with what we think about when we *compare* paychecks. Sticking to the usual scale, a dollar is a dollar, no matter the level of income. Making $1,001,000 is "worth" $1,000 more than making $1,000,000, and the intrinsic value of this difference is the same as that between incomes of $2,000 and $1,000. Both are differences of $1,000 — the base level does not matter. Working with logs is different. Working on a log scale implies that it's percentage change that matters. Thus, going from $1,000,000 to $1,001,000 is not very meaningful, whereas going from $1,000 to $2,000 is a huge difference. Indeed, when most of us think about a pay increase or salary negotiation, we think of it in terms of percentage change, not absolute change.

Class 3.   Sources of Variation

Why do data vary? When we measure GMAT scores, stock prices, or executive compensation, why don't we get a constant value for each? Much of the statistical analysis of data focuses upon discovering sources of variation in data.

Variation arises for many reasons. Often groups of values can be clustered into subsets identified by some qualitative factor such as industry type, and we can see that the resulting clusters have different properties. Quantitative factors also can be used to explain variation, and much of the material in the following course concerns methods for doing so.

Most of this class is devoted to analyzing data that flow in over time. Quite often a crucial source of variation is the passage of time. Much of the total variation over a period of time frequently arises from a time trend or seasonal pattern. In the context of quality control, variation arises from the inherent capability of the process as well as from special factors that influence the properties of the output. We will continue our analysis of control charts in the next class.

Topics
    Sources of variation
    Multiple boxplots
    Trends and seasonality
    Statistical independence; random variation versus systematic pattern
    Probability calculations
    Capable and in-control processes

Examples
    Variation by industry in executive compensation
    Patterns in early international airline passenger data
    Monitoring an automotive manufacturing process

Key Application

Seasonal trends. Most economic time series follow seasonal patterns. Housing
    construction in the US, for example, naturally slows down during the winter months as

weather conditions make it difficult to work outside. Knowing the presence of such
seasonal variation is very important. If an investor saw that the December housing
starts index was much lower than that for November, this information might lead the
investor to buy or sell different stocks since housing starts are a widely used economic
barometer of future trends. However, might this decay from November to December
be part of a "usual" reaction to worsening weather rather than an important leading
indicator? Answering this question would require one to look back and see what
typically happens during these months. To help people in this situation, many of these
economic series are "seasonally adjusted," corrected for the usual annual cycles. Thus,
when such an adjusted index drops, it's more likely to be economically meaningful.

Definitions

Trend. A systematic movement of the data over time. Most often we think of trends
occurring when data grow or fall steadily over an extended time period, but other trends
are more cyclic in nature, like those related to seasonal variation.

Seasonal variation. Variation in data that is often of a cyclical nature due to annual
fluctuations. One can also find cycles of shorter duration, such as catalog sales that
tend to be high on Monday and fall as the week progresses.

In-control process. A process is said to be "in control" if it shows no trend in either its
mean or its variability. A plot of the process against time should look like a random
swarm of points.

Capable process. A process is called "capable" if its mean and standard deviation meet the
design specifications.

Concepts

Sources of variation (also called sources of variability). Another way of thinking about
"sources of variation" is to understand them as reasons why the data we observe are not
constant. Take as an example the weekly sales of a ski store in Colorado. A year's
worth of weekly data would give us 52 data points. It seems exceptionally unlikely that
every week would have exactly the same level of sales. When one talks about sources
of variation, one is trying to explain why the weekly sales are not constant.

Perhaps the most obvious reason for variation in sales is that the ski season is seasonal, so one would expect more sales in the winter than in the summer. There may also be a holiday effect, with many people saving their shopping for regular sales. Both are examples of sources of variation. When you try to explain the sources of variation in data, you are implicitly starting to make a model. The sources of variation are likely to be considered as factors in a model which help us to predict weekly sales. Obviously, we would obtain a better prediction of weekly sales if we knew whether the week we are trying to predict is in the summer or the winter or whether a special sale was to occur.

The ability to pin down sources of variability is something that often comes with expert knowledge. Say we are going to try to predict aluminum futures. If you happen to know that a large proportion of new aluminum is used to make soda cans and that it's been a mild summer (so relatively fewer cans have been made), then you are in a position to make a better predictive model than your competition, assuming they have not reached the same conclusion.

Statistical independence. (This is a hard one!) Heuristically we can call two events "independent" if knowing the outcome of one gives you no additional information about the outcome of the other. For example, two "fair" coin tosses are independent; knowing the first coin was a head does not affect the chances of the second toss being a head (a fact that many gamblers do not understand). Returns for consecutive days on the stock market are typically not independent. What happens on Monday often influences what happens the following Tuesday.

A great simplifying feature of independence is that it leads to a simple rule for combining probabilities: if events A and B are independent, then the probability that A happens and that B happens is just the probability of A multiplied by the probability of B. The probability of heads on the first toss and heads on the second toss is just $1/2 \times 1/2 = 1/4$. If two events are not independent, then it is not correct to multiply the probabilities together.

The opposite of independence is "dependence." Dependence is also an important concept. The fact that there is dependence in the movements of certain stocks allows one to build a portfolio that can reduce risk.

Heuristics

Does the information add? (a guide for independence/effective sample size)

Another way of thinking about independence is through the accrual of information. You might intuitively think that if you have two data points, then you have twice as much information as contained in a single data point. In fact, this is only true if the data are independent. We will see an explicit formula that reflects the accumulation of information later in Class 4 (the formula is known as the standard error of the mean).

As an example, consider the information in two IQ measurements. You would expect to have twice as much information about the population mean IQ than if you had only one observation. If I tell you that the two IQ measurements are on identical twins, you may change your mind because you suspect that knowing the IQ of one twin gives you information about the other's IQ. It is as if the information overlaps between the two observations; it doesn't simply add up because IQ data on twins is dependent.

Potential Confusers

Being capable versus being in control.

Being capable refers to engineering considerations, implying that the process meets its design specs, whereas being in control is a statistical issue. The process can be in control but absolutely hopeless from a practical perspective. Simply put, it consistently produces output that is not adequate.

Variation by Industry in Executive Compensation

FrbSubst.jmp

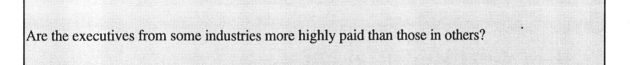

Are the executives from some industries more highly paid than those in others?

This example returns to the *Forbes* executive compensation data introduced in Class 2. For this example, to enhance the graphics, we have restricted attention to 10 broadly defined industries identified using the codes in the column labeled *Wide Industry*. A table of the number of executives from each of these industries appears next.

Wide Industry

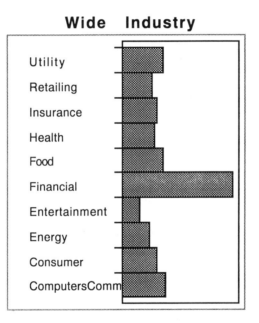

Frequencies

Industry	Count	Probability	Cum Prob
ComputersComm	67	0.10601	0.10601
Consumer	54	0.08544	0.19146
Energy	42	0.06646	0.25791
Entertainment	27	0.04272	0.30063
Financial	168	0.26582	0.56646
Food	62	0.09810	0.66456
Health	49	0.07753	0.74209
Insurance	54	0.08544	0.82753
Retailing	46	0.07278	0.90032
Utility	63	0.09968	1.00000
Total	632		

The distribution of total compensation is still quite skewed for the 623 executives who head companies in these 10 industries. Transformation of the compensation data to a log (base 10) scale (found in the calculator under *Transcendental*) avoids the compression due to the extreme skewness. (No, Eisner is not in this subset — Disney is not classified as an entertainment company!)

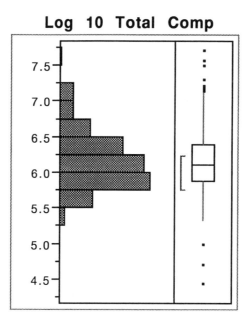

Log 10 Total Comp

Quantiles

maximum	100.0%	7.7252
quartile	75.0%	6.3940
median	50.0%	6.1096
minimum	0.0%	4.4596

Moments

Mean	6.1633
Std Dev	0.4117
N	623

How much of this variation in compensation can we attribute to differences among the industries? One way to see how total compensation varies by industry is to use plot linking. If we select a bin in the histogram showing the industries, the distribution of compensation for that group is highlighted in the histogram of (the log of) compensation.

Selecting the utility industry gives the following linked views

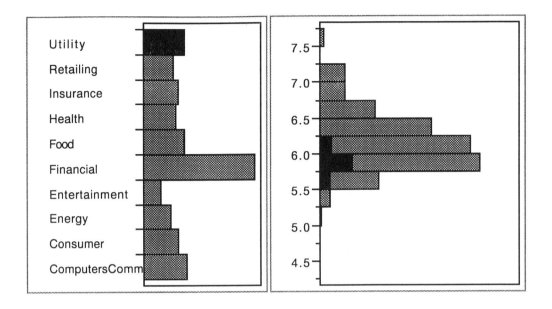

whereas selecting the computers/communication industry gives what appears to be a collection of higher compensation packages.

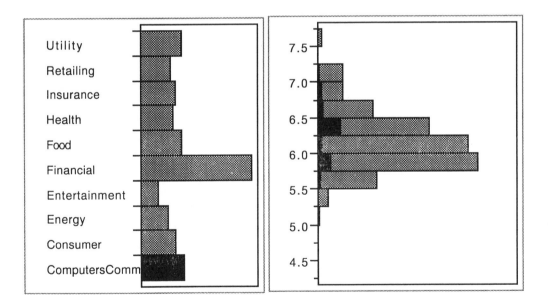

It's hard to make many of these comparisons since the groups appear to overlap. A better plot makes these comparisons in one image.

Some of the variation from one executive to another can be explained by the industry that employs each. Using the *Fit Y by X* command from the *Analyze* menu, we get the following comparison boxplots of the logged compensation data across the industries. The width of a box is proportional to the number of observations in the category. The financial industry contributes the most executives to this data set and hence has the widest box.

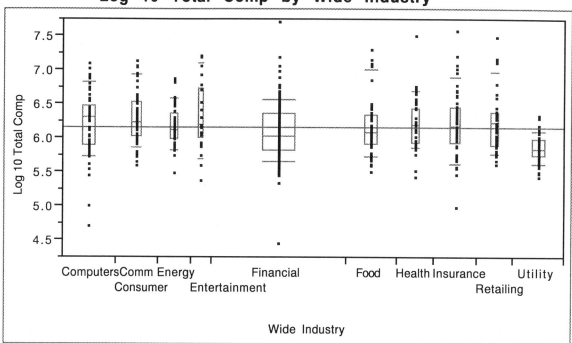

The median of the utility industry appears at the bottom, and the computer/communication industry seems to pay the most (judging by medians indicated by the centers of the boxes). The differences among the centers of the boxes, however, seem small relative to the variation within each industry. Relative to the dispersion within the industries, the differences among the medians (indicated by the center lines in the boxplots) do not seem very large; similarly, the boxplots show considerable overlap. Clearly, not everyone in a given industry is paid the same amount.

Are the executives from some industries more highly paid than those in others?

Some of the variation in compensation is explained by industry, but quite a bit of variation in total compensation remains within each of these 10 broadly defined industries — just consider the range within the financial industry.

Patterns in Early International Airline Passenger Data

IntlAir.jmp

Airlines, like most other businesses, need to anticipate the level of demand for their product. In particular, airlines need to anticipate the amount of passenger traffic in order to plan equipment leases and purchases. This problem becomes harder during periods of rapid growth in an expanding industry.

Based on the data from 1949 through 1960, what would you predict for January 1961?

A simple approach to getting a prediction for 1961 is based on combining the data for these 12 years and using the mean (280) or median (266) level of traffic. Since this is a time series, making a prediction from the histogram is foolish since it ignores the obvious trend.

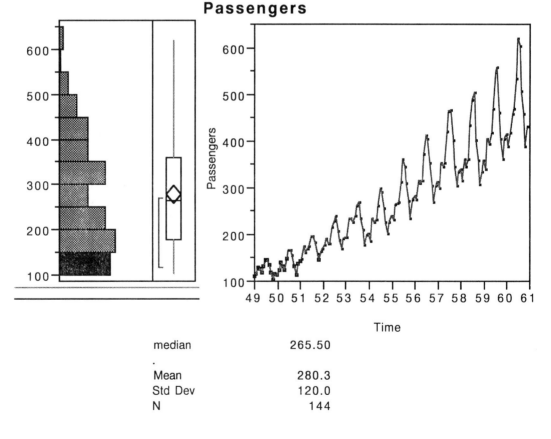

median	265.50
Mean	280.3
Std Dev	120.0
N	144

Alternatively, we can use relative changes as we did when we looked at the GM stock prices and base a prediction upon the relative change from month to month in the passenger traffic. Here is the formula. Pay particular attention to the subscripts. *Passengers* without a subscript is the same as *Passengers*$_i$,

$$\frac{Passengers - Passengers_{i-1}}{Passengers_{i-1}}$$

In comparison to the passenger traffic, very little trend appears in the relative changes.

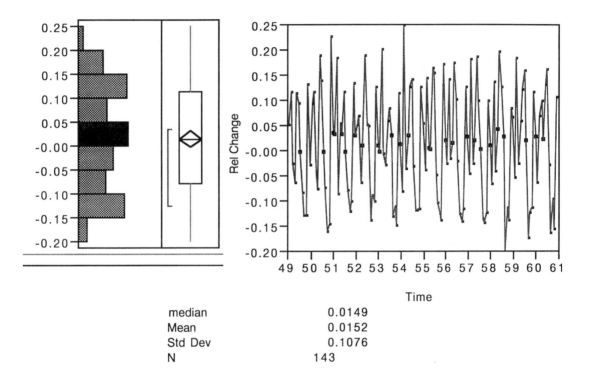

median	0.0149
Mean	0.0152
Std Dev	0.1076
N	143

Since there is little evident trend, using a summary like the mean makes a lot more sense here than with the original passenger data. The monthly increase (via either the mean or the median) is about 1.5%. Since the last observation for December 1960 is 432, a prediction based on the average relative change is

$$prediction = 432 \times 1.015 \approx 438 \,,$$

which seems much more reasonable than the mean level of passengers. Have we omitted anything?

Do any seasonal patterns remain? The plot of the original series clearly shows seasonality, with the variation increasing along with the level of passenger traffic.

P l o t

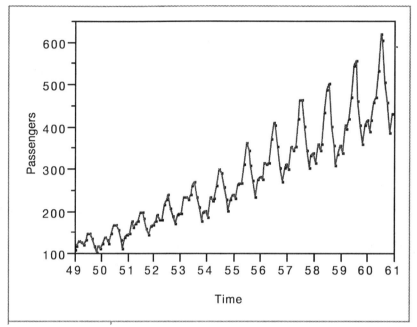

What happens for the relative changes? The previous plot appears, at least at first, to show no real trend. However, the linked plots below show a clear seasonal structure, only not as obvious as in the original data. On the left is a "histogram" of month with September selected (the months appear in reverse alphabetical order), and on the right is the plot of relative changes. All the relative changes for September are negative and seem to trend downward.

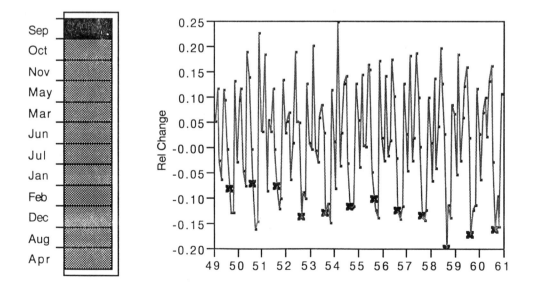

We can get a better idea of the size of the seasonal oscillations in the relative changes by grouping them by month. The following plot makes the seasonal structure of the changes quite clear. For example, the relative change in passenger traffic from December to January (shown by the boxplot on the left of the plot) is right around the average, whereas the traffic grows by quite a bit in December relative to November. (This plot is generated by the *Fit Y by X* command, exploiting a "subtle" feature of JMP. Grouping by *Month* does not work since JMP then orders the data alphabetically, with April first. The *Month Code* variable works, but notice that it is declared as a ordinal variable. You can't get the nice boxplots without the x-variable being ordinal or nominal.)

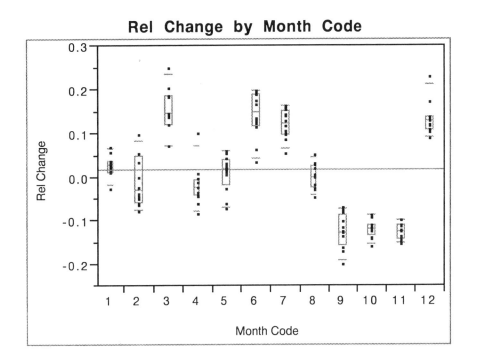

Since the typical growth from December to January (again, the boxplot on the extreme left of the plot) is near the average, it seems the analyst got lucky and our prediction based on the average overall relative change ought to be reasonable, even though we had not noted the exposed seasonal patterns. Given the seasonality, a somewhat better prediction would be to use the median or average of this first boxplot; the median growth is 3% and the average growth is 2.6%.

Although this plot does make the seasonal patterns more evident, notice that it conceals any evidence of a time trend for the data within a month (like that which we noticed in the plot of the September data).

Airlines, like most other businesses, need to anticipate the level of demand for their product. In particular, airlines need to anticipate the amount of passenger traffic in order to plan equipment leases and purchases.

Based on the data from 1949 through 1960, what would you predict for January 1961?

The prediction of 438 based on the average relative change captures the growth in the airline business during these years and is much more reasonable than that using the average level of traffic. The prediction based on relative changes is also not weakened by the seasonal patterns in this data since the typical January increase is near the overall average increase.

A general theme of this analysis is that by re-expressing the data as relative changes, we have removed much of the trend. Now we don't have to forecast the trend, just pick the typical value from the collection of relative changes.

As always, alternative approaches abound. One particularly simple approach is to focus on just the data for January. In this case, a relatively simple trend model will do the trick. Unfortunately, such a model does not use any of the information in the other $^{11}/_{12}$ of the data. Regression models that you'll study later let you "borrow strength," combining data where they are similar while still allowing for differences where they are important.

Many types of more specialized models have been developed for modeling time series. We barely scratch the surface of time series analysis. The data used in this example come from a very well-known text on time series analysis, that of Box and Jenkins (*Time Series Analysis: Forecasting and Control*, Holden-Day, 1976). This time series has become a benchmark for evaluating new forecasting methodologies.

Monitoring an Automotive Manufacturing Process

ShaftDia.jmp

In order for assembled automobile engines to perform properly, the main motor shaft diameter used to build the engine must be within the range of 810 to 820 thousandths of an inch.

Does the current process meet this standard? Has the process been steady over time, or do day-of-the-week effects and trend affect the data?

The theme of this example is that when we have a sequence of observations without trend, we can use summary statistics computed from these data to monitor the consistency of a manufacturing process (or any type of process, for that matter). The process being studied produces motor shafts that are used to build car engines. Data have been sampled from this process at a selected engine-building plant. Shafts were sampled over a period of four weeks, with five shafts sampled each weekday (Monday to Friday), giving a total of 100 measurements.

We ultimately want to install a system for monitoring production in the future to ensure that future process output — the collection of all motor shafts — is meeting standards. As long as sampled data from the process lie within an acceptable range (to be determined), the monitoring system concludes that the process is functioning properly. When data from the process fall outside this range (i.e., shafts are either too small or too large), the system concludes that the process is no longer functioning properly. The challenge is to define such limits. Should we use individual shaft measurements, or perhaps some type of summary? Whatever the choice, most monitoring systems must be able to check the process without the expense of having to measure every shaft that comes off the line.

The first step of this task is to verify that the available data are representative of an acceptable, consistent process. Once we have done so, we need to choose a decision rule for deciding that the process is okay.

The histogram of the 100 motor shafts gathered over the four weeks shows that indeed all of the shaft diameters fall well within the production guidelines. A process whose output falls within the designated acceptance limits is said to be *capable*. We also need to check that the process is *in control*. A process is in control if the data show no systematic trend. For this example, the process is in control if the distribution of the shaft diameters is consistent through time. The plots indicate that this process is both in control as well as capable.

Shaft   Diameter

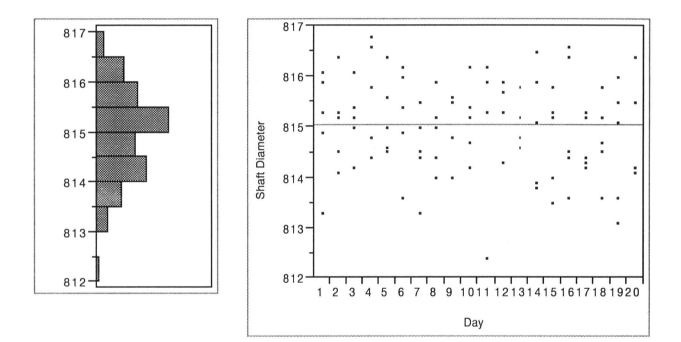

Thus far, we have a good idea of what's going on with these 100 shafts. However, what can we say about the process? Remember, our goal is not simply to check these 100 shafts, but rather to make a claim about the *underlying process* producing all of the shafts. For example, what is our best estimate of a shaft diameter falling outside of the control limits sometime in the future,

$$Pr(\text{diameter} < 810 \quad OR \quad \text{diameter} > 820) = ?$$

Without some additional assumptions, we can go no further than simply to say that this event has not happened among the 100 shafts we have seen.

Since the process is both capable and in control, these data are representative of the process output. If we also assume normality, we can compute this probability using the mean (815 mils) and SD (0.89 mils) of these shafts. Assuming these characteristics are close to those for the underlying process, the event of a shaft falling outside the tolerance limits is quite unlikely since either boundary is about 5.5 SDs away.

Before we carry these calculations very far, though, we need to check for normality rather than just assume it. The normal quantile plot shows that the normal model works very well with this data; all of the points in the plot in the right-hand frame lie within the allowed variation.

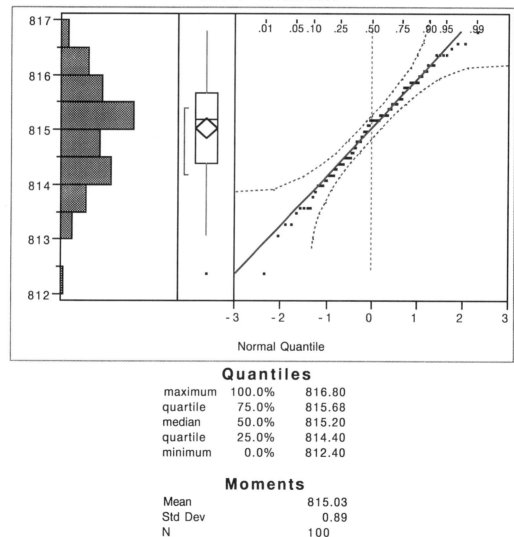

Shaft   Diameter

Normal Quantile

Quantiles

maximum	100.0%	816.80
quartile	75.0%	815.68
median	50.0%	815.20
quartile	25.0%	814.40
minimum	0.0%	812.40

Moments

Mean	815.03
Std Dev	0.89
N	100

Now we need to think about setting an acceptance range for monitoring the process in the future. Assuming that we are satisfied with the current process output indicated in this collection of 100 shafts, we need to set up a *statistical decision rule* that we can use to monitor the process to see that it keeps producing this kind of output. In quality control, statistical decision rules attempt to determine as quickly as possible when the process has gone out of control while at the same time avoid unnecessarily shutting down the process when in fact the process is still in control.

From the data on the individual shafts, the empirical rule suggests that when the process is under control, virtually all of the shafts should fall in the range

$$\bar{X} \pm 3 \text{ SD} = \mu \pm 3\sigma \approx 815 \pm 3 \, (.9) = [812.3, \, 817.7] \ .$$

Thus, as shafts are sampled, finding one whose diameter lies outside of this range indicates one of two things:

   (1) we saw one of those rare values that occasionally happen — a "miracle", or
   (2) the process is no longer functioning as designed.

Our decision rule is to act as though the second implication holds and to conclude that the process has changed.

Since we are going to conclude that the process has gone *out of control* when a value falls outside of this range (and presumably take some corrective action), it's a good idea to make sure that not too many miracles are likely to happen. We do not want to unnecessarily shut down the process too often. Probability calculations are very handy to find the answer. *Assuming* that the data are normal (which seems reasonable here), the empirical rule indicates that

$$\text{Pr(randomly chosen shaft diameter } within \text{ control limits)}$$
$$= \text{Pr} \, (\mu - 3\sigma \leq \text{ diameter } \leq \mu + 3 \, \sigma)$$
$$= 0.9973 \ .$$

So the chance of seeing such an unusual shaft while the process remains under control is pretty small,

$$\text{Pr(randomly chosen shaft diameter } outside \text{ control limits)} = 1 - 0.9973 = 0.0027 \ .$$

However, we typically want to examine many of the items that come off the assembly line, not just one. Suppose we will sample 100 new shafts coming off the line, 5 on each of the next 20 days (just like with our initial data). To figure out the answer now requires two more important assumptions, in addition to the assumption of normality:

(1) the shaft diameters come from the same normal process (that is, μ and σ are fixed), and

(2) the shaft diameters are independently drawn from the process.

Now the calculation of any one of these sampled shafts falling out of the control limits can be done, especially if you have a calculator with the y^x button:

$$
\begin{aligned}
\text{Pr(miracle)} \quad &= \text{Pr}(\textit{some} \text{ shaft outside control limits while under control}) \\
&= 1 - \text{Pr}(\textit{all} \text{ shafts inside control limits}) \\
&= 1 - \text{Pr}(\text{1st inside } \textit{AND} \text{ 2nd inside } \textit{AND} \text{ ... } \textit{AND} \text{ 100}^{\text{th}} \text{ inside}) \\
\text{(independent)} \quad &= 1 - \text{Pr (1st inside)} \times \text{Pr (2nd inside)} \times ... \times \text{Pr (100}^{\text{th}} \text{ inside)} \\
\text{(same)} \quad &= 1 - 0.9973 \times 0.9973 \times ... \times 0.9973 = 1 - 0.9973^{100} \\
&= 1 - 0.7631 \\
&= 0.2369 .
\end{aligned}
$$

Maybe miracles are more likely than we thought! In fact, some managers use control limits wider than $\mu \pm 3\sigma$ for just this reason. Wider limits reduce the chances for us to think that the process is out of control when it's not. But they achieve this at a price. What do you think happens to the chances of detecting an out-of-control process when we widen the control limits?

A related important idea that is useful to consider is what can we say about the probability of a shaft outside the limits *if the shafts were not independent*? Without independence, we cannot convert all of those "*ANDs*" into a big product. However, we can still get an idea of what's happening without making different assumptions. Namely, we can put an upper bound on the probability using what is known as *Bonferroni's inequality*:

$$
\begin{aligned}
\text{Pr (miracle)} \quad &= \text{Pr (}\textit{some} \text{ shaft outside control limits while under control)} \\
&= \text{Pr(1st outside } \textit{OR} \text{ 2nd outside } \textit{OR} \text{ ... } \textit{OR} \text{ 100}^{\text{th}} \text{ outside)} \\
\text{(Bonferroni)} \quad &\leq \text{Pr(1st outside) + Pr(2nd outside) + ... + Pr(100}^{\text{th}} \text{ outside)} \\
&= 0.0027 + 0.0027 + ... + 0.0027 = 100 \, (0.0027) \\
&= 0.27,
\end{aligned}
$$

which we can see is quite close in this illustration to the answer under independence.

Alternatively, why base a decision on individual shaft values? If we use daily averages rather than individual measurements, we have 20 averages, and thus the chance for some average randomly falling outside the ±3"σ" control limits is reduced to $1 - .9973^{20} = 0.053$ — about 5%. Notes at the end of the continuation of this example in Class 4 give some other advantages. However, if we decide to use averages of several shafts, how should we determine the acceptance region? What value do we use for "σ"?

Aggregating our original sample to the level of days and plotting on the scale of the raw data gives the following graph. (Don't worry about the error bars, we'll come to them shortly.)

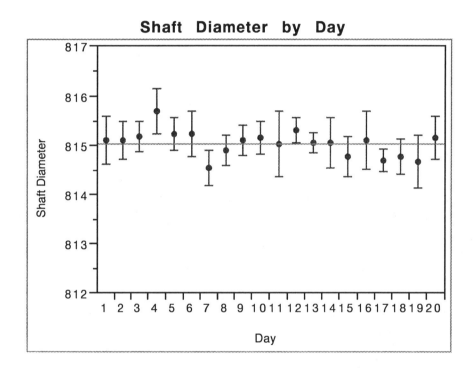

The 20 averages of the data occupy but a small part of the plot that once showed the actual data. The daily means are much less variable than the individual shafts.

JMP Hint

If you want to work with the daily averages rather than just plot them, you need to use the *Group/Summary* command from the *Tables* menu to generate a new data set. Pick *Day* as the group variable, select the *Shaft Diameter* column, and then select the mean (or other summary stats). You'll be rewarded with a new spreadsheet, aggregated as daily values.

Going one step further, we can aggregate the data up to weeks, combining the data from five days into one batch. The means of the 25 shafts sampled each week are much more consistent from one week to the next than the individual shaft measurements. That is, the mean of one batch of 25 shaft diameters is more likely to be close to the mean of another batch than are two randomly selected shafts likely to be close to each other.

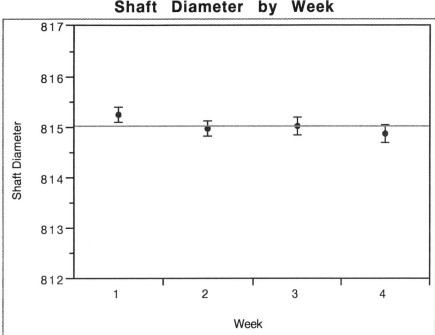

As we aggregate the diameters into longer time periods, the means become more consistent from one group to the next. The mean of one shaft diameter (the value itself) is more variable than the mean diameter of five shafts. The mean diameter of five shafts is more variable than the mean diameter of 25 shafts. Evidently, the mean becomes more stable as the size of the group increases, *assuming that the process is in control.*

The question that remains for us to resolve is how to put limits on the allowed values of the daily mean and standard deviation. Why these summaries? If we think that the normal model is reasonable, then we have lost little by compressing the data into these daily summaries since the mean and standard deviation completely characterize the normal curve. We will see how to do this in Class 4.

Do the diameters of these shafts indicate that the process meets the standard?

Has the process been steady over time?

We have determined that the process is capable (the shaft diameters are within the acceptance limits) and, by some informal comparisons, that the process is in control (the distribution of shaft diameters is relatively steady through time). For this first look at quality control, we have focused on the average. In the next class, we will see that it is important to look at the variability as well.

Now we have to settle how to establish rules for monitoring whether the process remains capable and under control. We have already noticed a crucial feature: means become less variable as the group size increases. We will continue with an expanded version of this analysis in the next class.

Six-Sigma Limits in Manufacturing

A related notion that you will often read about is the "six-sigma limits" terminology introduced by Motorola. These limits describe the design criteria, what we call the capability of the process, rather than the notion of being in control. The six-sigma limits indicate the probability that a manufactured item lies within the design tolerances. Suppose that we are producing electronic components, with a design spec of 10 units and a tolerance range of 7 to 13 units. If the SD of the manufacturing process is 1, then we have a three-sigma process, one that produces about 27 defectives per 10,000 items. If, on the other hand, the process SD = 0.5, then we have a six-sigma process with a minuscule 2 defectives per billion components. Here's a table of the relevant probabilities for various values of sigma:

Probability of Defective Component

2 sigma	0.045 5
3 sigma	0.002 7
4 sigma	0.000 063 3
5 sigma	0.000 000 573
6 sigma	0.000 000 001 97

Why the concern? Suppose that a cellular telephone uses 400 of these components. The chance of a phone working using 400 three-sigma components is only about 1 in 3:

$$\text{Pr(phone works)} = \text{Pr(}all\text{ components work)} = 0.9973^{400} = 0.339.$$

Thus, most of the phones that we have assembled will not work! (As in the previous examples, this calculation presumes normality as well as independence.) Switching to six-sigma components raises the probability of a phone working to nearly 1:

$$\text{Pr(Phone works)} = 0.999\ 999\ 99803^{400} = 0.999\ 999\ 2$$

These ideas are becoming more relevant and common in business. For example, the February 24, 1997, issue of *Financial Times* has an article about "a black belt in quality." Though they did not get the probabilities quite right (see page 7), the article discusses in the importance of six-sigma limits in manufacturing.

Class 4. Standard Error

Control charts are important tools for ensuring quality in manufacturing. This class shows how control charts are constructed and used to monitor various types of processes. The key idea in developing these charts combines the empirical rule from Class 2 with our observation that summary measures such as the mean vary less than the original data. How much less? Today we show how variation in the average, as measured by its standard error, is related to variation in the individual values. We then determine, with the help of the normal model and the empirical rule, how to set one type of control limits.

This is a hard class with some very important concepts that frequently appear in the rest of this course and throughout our subsequent development of regression methods.

Topics
>   Populations and samples
>   Parameters (population mean μ and variance σ^2) and their estimators
>   Standard error of the mean ($s/\sqrt{n}$ and $\sigma/\sqrt{n}$)
>   Control limits in quality-control charts; alternative rules
>   Central limit theorem

Examples
>   Control charts for motor shafts (continued)
>   Control chart analysis of car trunk seam variation
>   Analysis of production of computer chips

Key Applications

> *Quality and the standard error of the mean.* It may at times be more efficient to monitor a
> series of summary statistics concerning a process rather than the entire process itself.
> For example, a sequence of hourly measurements collected over a month may be
> compressed to daily means or even weekly means. The question then arises of how to
> estimate the variability of daily or weekly means based on the variability of the hourly
> raw data.

> *Value at risk.* Another example of the necessity to understand how variability accumulates
> is in the estimation of value at risk from daily earnings at risk. Value at risk is a more

appropriate measure of financial risk when the decision horizon is more than one day, but a similar question arises of how to use a daily risk calculation to obtain a weekly risk calculation.

Definitions

Population. The entire collection of objects that we wish to describe, such as all of the possible output of a manufacturing process.

Sample. A subset of the population. If the sample is the entire population, then the sample is called a "census."

Concepts

Standard error of the mean. The standard error of the mean is the standard deviation of the sample mean. Not surprisingly, means are less variable than individual observations. If we denote the sample standard deviation of an individual observation as s and base the mean on a sample of size n, then the standard error of the mean is $s/\sqrt{n}$. In contrast, totals are *more* variable than the individual items. The standard error of the total is $s\sqrt{n}$, n times larger.

The central limit theorem. The standard error of the mean relates the standard deviation of the mean of a set of observations to the standard deviation of the individual observations. The central limit theorem expands this relationship by stating that the sample mean itself approximately has a normal distribution provided that one has a large enough sample. This is true even if the raw data that comprise the sample are not from a normal distribution.

It is easy to overlook the utility of this fact. Since it implies that sample means obey the empirical rule, we know a lot about a sample mean before being observed. For example, even though the sampled population is not normal, we can apply the empirical rule to means from samples of this population and predict that a new sample mean will lie within $\mu \pm 2\, s/\sqrt{n}$ 95% of the time.

Heuristic

Means are less variable than observations. Means become less variable as the sample size increases; divide s by $\sqrt{n}$ to get their SE. Totals, on the other hand, become more variable, so multiply s by $\sqrt{n}$ to obtain the correct SE.

Potential Confusers

Notation. To distinguish features of the process from those of a sample, a special notation is common. Greek letters typically describe features of the process or population, and Latin counterparts denote the sample analogs.

	Population Feature	Sample Characteristic
Mean	μ	$\bar{X}$
Standard deviation (SD)	σ	s
Variance	σ^2	s^2

σ *versus s.* σ is the standard deviation in the population that has been sampled, whereas s is the standard deviation of an observed sample. If we have a large sample, the distinction is not too important since $\sigma \approx s$ in this case.

Sampling variation and standard error. The fact that sample means themselves are variable is often a difficult idea to grasp. There are at least two ways to think about this. One is to recognize that the sample you selected is just one of many possible samples that could have been chosen. A different sample would have given a different sample mean; the mean varies from one sample to another. A second way of thinking about it is to anticipate what the sample mean is going to be before you have collected the data. You don't know it, making it uncertain and hence variable.

Control Charts for Motor Shafts

ShaftXtr.jmp

What rules should be used to monitor the motor shaft process to ensure that the process remains under control?

Our previous analysis of the motor shaft diameters indicated that the process was both capable and in control. In this example, we construct rules that employees can use to monitor the process to see that it maintains this past level of performance. The key idea is to establish limits for the amount of variation in observed summary measures when the process is under control.

We also learned in the previous class that the control limits for acceptance rules depend on the number of observations that are combined into a summary like the mean. Similar rules can be developed for other summaries as well. Though we won't go into the details, we'll also use a rule that monitors the SD of the process over time as well.

For this analysis, a larger sample of 400 motor shafts is used; the first 100 of these were considered in the last example of Class 3. The following sequence plot suggests that the process is still in control and capable.

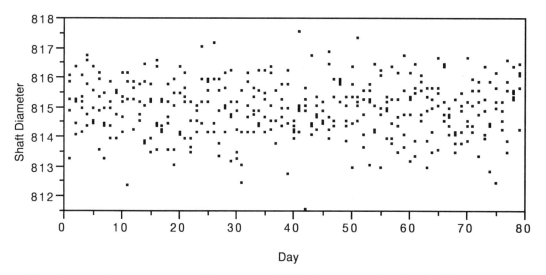

The plots on the next page are histograms of this data at varying levels of aggregation, beginning with the top histogram of 400 shaft diameters, then daily means, and last the weekly means. As noted previously, the means are less variable in the larger groups.

A JMP option shows histograms horizontally; use the *Group/Summary* item from the *Tables* menu to construct the needed summary stats.

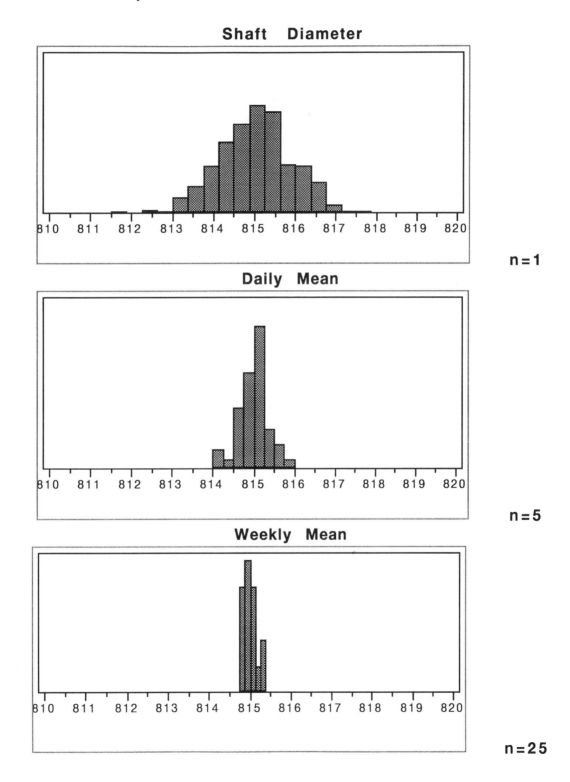

The associated summary statistics summarize these distributions. The mean stays the same regardless of the level of aggregation; the centers of the prior three histograms are the same. In contrast, note the steady decrease of the observed standard deviations, which are marked with an arrow.

Raw diameters

Quantiles

maximum	100.0%	817.60
quartile	75.0%	815.60
median	50.0%	815.05
quartile	25.0%	814.40
minimum	0.0%	811.60

Moments

Mean	814.99	
Std Dev	**0.93**	⇐
N	400	shafts

Daily averages

Quantiles

maximum	100.0%	815.98
quartile	75.0%	815.22
median	50.0%	815.00
quartile	25.0%	814.76
minimum	0.0%	814.18

Moments

Mean	814.9918	
Std Dev	**0.36**	⇐
	80	daily means

Weekly averages

Quantiles

maximum	100.0%	815.30
quartile	75.0%	815.09
median	50.0%	814.97
quartile	25.0%	814.87
minimum	0.0%	814.79

Moments

Mean	814.9917	
Std Dev	**0.15**	⇐
	16	weekly means

A plot of the observed standard deviation against the associated number of observations in each group suggests that the SD of the group average drops as the group size increases, but at a decreasing rate. As the number *n* of shafts that are averaged increases, the SD of the means goes down.

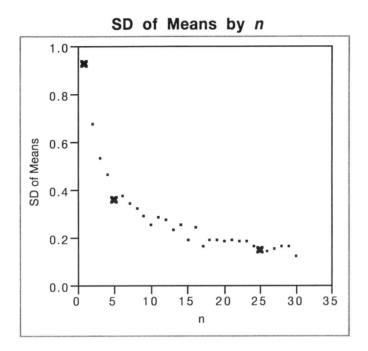

The three points marked with an "x" in this figure are the SDs highlighted on the previous page. The others were calculated (though not with JMP) to fill in the gaps.

A very smooth curve (constructed using a curve-fitting procedure known as simple regression discussed in Class 11) describes the relationship between the standard deviation of the means and the group size *n* quite well.

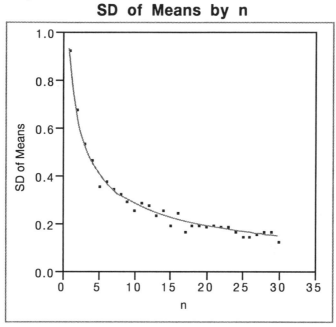

It can be shown mathematically that, if the process is in control, the standard deviation of the group average drops off at a rate inversely proportional to the square root of the sample size (group size). The standard deviation of the sample mean is also known as the *standard error of the mean* (to distinguish this measure of variation from the standard deviation of an observation). As a formula, we have

$$\text{SD(mean of } n \text{ observations)} = \text{standard error of the mean} = \frac{\text{constant}}{\sqrt{n}} \text{ ,}$$

where *n* denotes the associated sample size. The constant term is actually the standard deviation of one observation produced by the process, which we have denoted by σ. The expression for the standard error of the mean is thus

$$\text{SE(mean of } n \text{ observations)} = \frac{\text{SD(one observation)}}{\sqrt{n}} = \frac{\sigma}{\sqrt{n}} \text{ .}$$

Of course, the formula $\sigma/\sqrt{n}$ is impractical since we almost never know the true process standard deviation σ. All we usually have is the sample standard deviation s, and we can use it as an estimate of the process standard deviation σ. This substitution gives a practical formula for estimating the standard error of a mean of n observations:

$$\text{SE(mean of } n \text{ observations)} = \frac{\text{SD(one observation)}}{\sqrt{n}} = \frac{\sigma}{\sqrt{n}} \approx \frac{s}{\sqrt{n}}$$

Now that we have a handle on how the variation of group averages is related to group size, we can define a procedure for monitoring a process. In the ideal context in which data follow a normal distribution, the empirical rule gives us the following:

Interval	*Proportion of data within interval*	
$\mu \pm \sigma$	.6827 $\approx$ 2/3	
$\mu \pm 2\sigma$	.9544 $\approx$ 19/20	
$\mu \pm 3\sigma$	.9973,	nearly everything
$\mu \pm 4\sigma$	.999 936 6,	closer to everything!
$\mu \pm 5\sigma$	.999 999 43,	what's left now?
$\mu \pm 6\sigma$	.999 999 998 03,	"six-sigma"

We used this rule in Class 2 as a way of showing, for normal data, that the mean and the standard deviation provide a rather complete characterization of the distribution of the observed data that have a normal distribution. Now we are going to use this rule to set limits for a control chart.

What we need are limits, both upper and lower, for the daily average. Values outside such a range will indicate that the process is no longer functioning properly and must be shut down and repaired. The empirical rule suggests a means for setting these limits, and the probability calculations at the end of Class 3 offer some caveats to the usual rule of being within plus or minus three standard errors of the process mean. A similar argument works for the standard deviation as well, allowing us to track the two key summary measures of location and spread.

The next page shows the control charts produced by JMP. To check our understanding of what has happened, we will do a few illustrative calculations. From prior pages, we have these summary statistics:

	Individual Shafts	Daily Averages(n=5)
Mean	815	815
Std Dev	0.93	0.36
N	400	80

To set the limits for the daily averages, we have two choices. The naive choice is to use the SD of the 80 averages we computed from the 400 shafts, obtaining the upper control limit (with a similar rule used to set the LCL, or lower control limit)

$$UCL = 815 \; + \; 3 \, (0.36) \; = 816.08 \; .$$

This is reasonable, but it's better (meaning more efficient) to use all 400 shafts and our *formula* for the standard error of a mean. Namely, replace the SD of the observed 80 means by

$$SE(mean) = \frac{SD \; obs}{\sqrt{5}} = \frac{0.93}{\sqrt{5}} = 0.42 \; .$$

The upper limit in the next figure is thus set by the calculation (the value in the figure is 816.29 because of rounding)

$$UCL = 815 + 3 \, (0.42) \approx 816.26 \; .$$

Why is this better? When we used the 80 shaft averages, we were in effect estimating the SE via a small "simulation," as though we did not know the formula. The formula lets us use the information in all 400 shafts rather than just the 80 averages and thus is more precise.

With the data grouped by day, the mean control chart is the following.

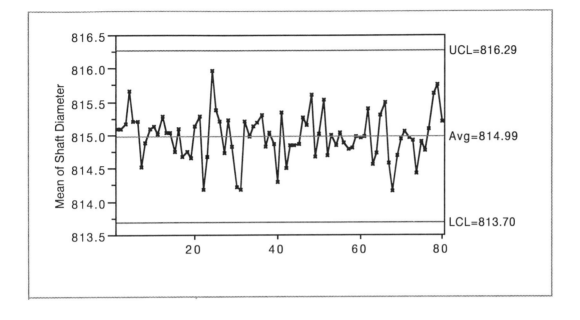

With the data grouped instead by week, we obtain the following plot. Note that the control limits are different. The standard error is smaller since the batch size is 25 when grouped by week.

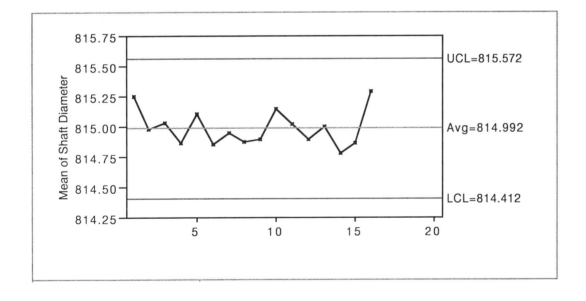

We also need to look at the S-charts that show the standard deviation for each day

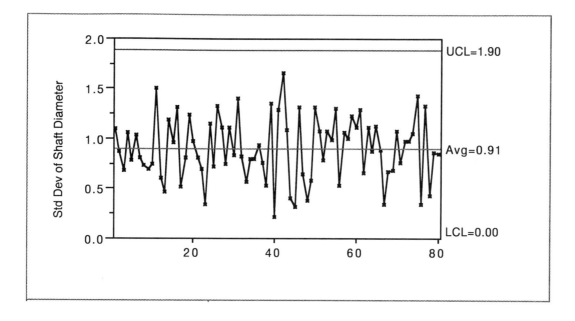

and for each week (the chart below). In either case, the process is under control.

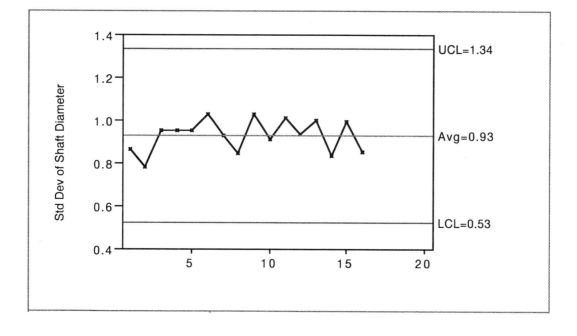

How should we establish rules for monitoring the motor shaft process to ensure that the process remains under control?

If we set control limits using the empirical rule and the relationship of the SE of the mean to the SD of an observation, we obtain limits for two crucial summary measures: the mean and the standard deviation of the process. When values cross these bounds, we have strong reason to suspect that the process is no longer under control and needs repair.

Comments:

(1) The limits for such a process are often set externally to meet design specifications, as suggested in the discussion of six-sigma limits following the notes for Class 3.

(2) The process might go out of control and still remain within these limits. Imagine the mean values regularly cycling up and down, yet staying within the allowed bounds. Staying within the bounds does not necessarily mean that the process is under control.

(3) Other rules exists for interpreting QC charts. The JMP manual discusses some of these variations which are also available in the software. Watch out, though, when reading other sources on quality control because the numbering of these tests is not standard.

Some Details

So why group the data into means? Why not just look at one shaft at a time rather than form averages? There are several reasons:

(1) The variation of means is better characterized by normality (CLT),

(2) The reduction in the number of comparisons reduces the chances of "false positives", and

(3) Averages make it possible to detect small changes in the process mean.

We have considered (1) and (2) in the previous discussions; here is an example of (3).

To make the calculations easier, let's assume that the initial process mean when all is well is 815 and the SD of individual shafts is 1,

$$\mu = 815, \; \sigma = 1.$$

The control interval for inspecting one shaft at a time is then

$$\text{one shaft} \qquad [815 \pm 3] = [812, 818].$$

With $n = 4$ shafts, the SE(mean of 4) $= {}^1/\sqrt{4} = {}^1/2$, so that the interval is

$$\text{four shafts} \qquad [815 \pm 3/2] \; = [813.5, 816.5].$$

Now consider what happens if the process mean shifts upward from 815, becoming larger by wear or some other failure, to 816 mils. *How long will it take for us to detect this change?*

Looking at one shaft at a time, we can calculate the probability of a shaft's exceeding the upper control limit. Since the mean is now 816, the upper limit is 2 SDs away. Thus, the probability of exceeding this upper limit once the process has changed increases to about

$$({}^1/2) \, ({}^1/20) = {}^1/40 \, .$$

This probability suggests by some related calculations that we expect to examine 40 shafts before we find one that exceeds the limit. Quite a few get by before we realize that the process has changed. By comparison, the chance of a mean of four shafts' exceeding the upper limit for averages is much larger,

$$\text{Pr(mean of four shafts} > 816.5 \,) = \text{Pr(normal} > 1 \text{ SD above its mean}) \approx 1/6.$$

Thus, we expect to have to inspect 6 means of four shafts before encountering one that tells us that the process has changed. That's only $6 \times 4 = 24$ shafts before we expect to detect the problem, and consequently *a much faster detection procedure than looking at one at a time.* Using sample means rather than individual values provides a faster way to detect small shifts in the process mean.

We can compute a graph that shows the optimal group size to detect a mean shift of one SD, as in this example. The best group size seems to be slightly larger than 10.

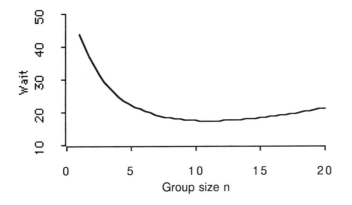

Reality is seldom so simple. Suppose that the process mean shifts by 2 SDs rather than just one. Now using big groups becomes a liability. Here is the corresponding chart. A group size of only 2 or 3 appears best.

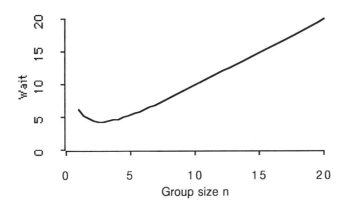

The reason, then, for using a mean of several shafts rather than just one is that the use of an average leads to a more *sensitive* procedure. If we are concerned about detecting small changes in the process, we need to use an average rather than track individual values. The optimal number to use in forming the average depends on the size of the change we need to detect.

Control Chart Analysis of Car Trunk Seam Variation

CarSeam.jmp

Specifications of an auto manufacturer call for a trunk seam width of 0.300 cm, with an allowable standard deviation of 0.060 cm. Are the trunks of vehicles coming off the assembly line meeting these specifications?

The manufacturer collected data on the width in centimeters of the seam at the upper left corner of the trunk of a car on the assembly line. Consistency in seam width is an important measure of the quality of manufacturing (think of those TV ads with the marble or ball bearing rolling around the seam of the car).

To obtain the data used in this example, each day the manufacturer sampled 10 cars at random from the assembly line. The experiment continued for 62 consecutive work days, with seven days per week. A total of 620 seam widths was thus obtained. The sampling was performed to determine if production is meeting specifications, and to assist in making appropriate modifications to the production process when such action is necessary.

The following sequence plot shows no clear time trends, indicating that we can check for the normality of the data via a quantile plot.

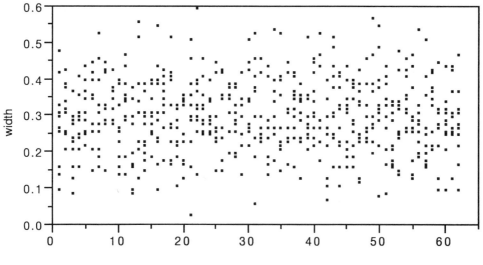

The marginal distribution of the 620 seam widths appears normal, with no extreme outliers or skewness evident. We still need to look sequentially for trends.

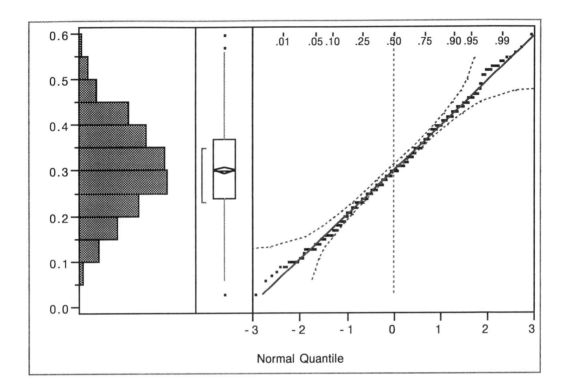

The X-bar chart and the S-chart focus on the summary statistics for each batch of numbers, here the 10 observations for each day. The X-bar chart is a plot of average daily width versus time, with the mean and standard deviation from given specifications. In contrast to the previous example, the chart uses the given process specifications to determine the control limits. The center line is the specified target seam width, and the upper and lower limits are three target standard deviations of the mean away from this value. The upper control limit for the daily means, for example, is determined by using the input values $\mu = 0.3$ for the mean and $\sigma = 0.06$, giving

$$\text{upper limit} = \mu + 3 \; \sigma/\sqrt{10} \; = 0.3 + 3 \; (0.06/\sqrt{10} \;) = 0.357 \; .$$

Considered a day at a time in the next two control charts, some of the daily averages are below the lower control limit. About half of the daily standard deviations are too large. The points that are highlighted in these two control charts are those associated with the highlighted week in the next two charts which show the weekly summaries. This simultaneous highlighting is very useful in many cases such as this to see which points are associated between several plots. When using JMP with control charts at different levels of aggregation, the plot-linking feature shows which observations are combined. The highlighted week in the previous charts leads to seven highlighted observations in the charts of the daily summaries.

Looking at the data grouped by week makes it hard to tell if some of the variation is occurring within the week. It also means that we have to wait until the end of the week to detect a problem. Notice also how much less variable the weekly means are compared to the daily means on the facing page. Averaging the 70 points in a week has greatly reduced the variation, as we expect from our discussion of standard error.

Either S chart makes it clear that the process is consistently exceeding the upper control limit for its variation. The process is clearly *not capable* of meeting the required standards for production. (It may, however, be in control since the distribution has not changed much over these nine weeks of data.)

Daily Charts

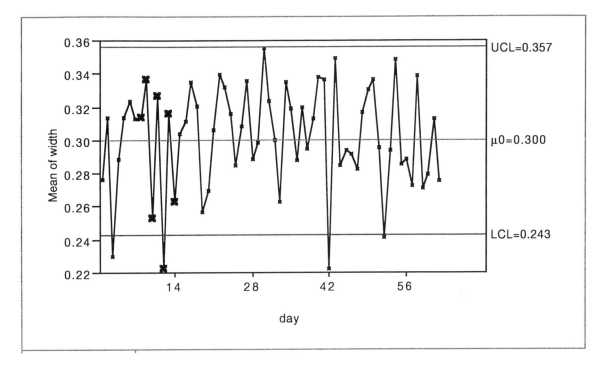

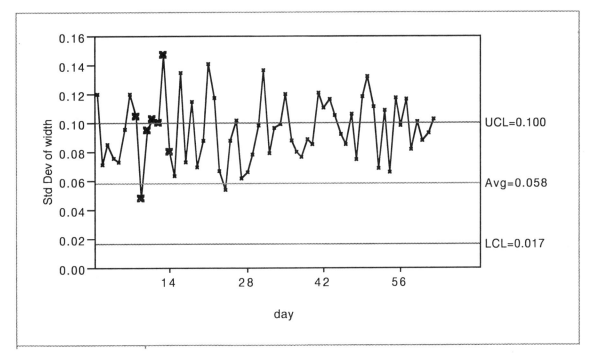

Weekly Charts

The limits widen for the last week since it only includes 6 rather than 7 days. Values are not given for the limits since the limits change for the last week (which is not complete).

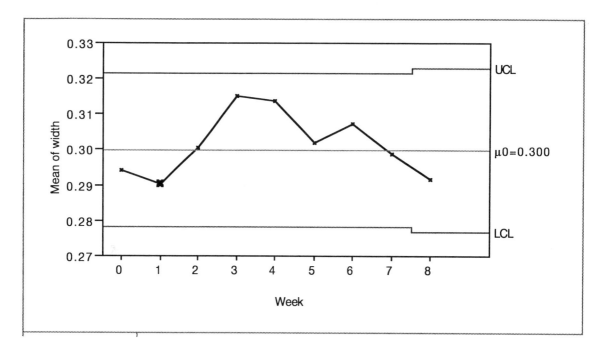

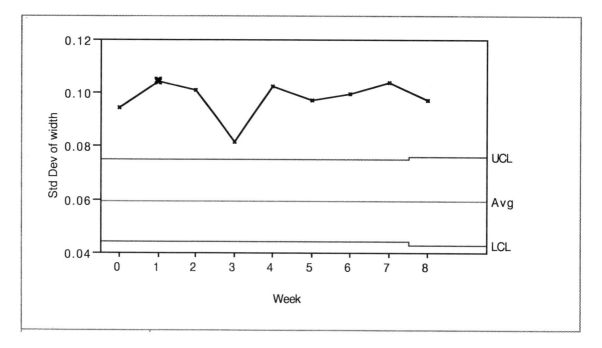

> Specifications for an auto manufacturer call for a trunk seam width of 0.300 cm, with an allowable standard deviation of 0.060 cm. Are the trunks of vehicles coming off the assembly line meeting these specifications?

The variation is much larger than the target specification. As a result, the seams occasionally are much too wide or much too narrow; the process is not capable. The deviations from the standards are consistent throughout the time period of observation and have not come about from some sudden change in the underlying process. Thus we have a process which seems in control, but the performance is not capable of meeting the desired specifications.

In the previous motor shaft example, the specifications do not give the target standard deviation. The standard deviation is estimated from the data and used to set the control limits. In this example (and the next on computer chips), the specifications set both the target mean *and* standard deviation.

Some Alternative Control Charts

Before leaving the car seam data, let's consider another aspect of control charts. Suppose that the specifications had been for a mean width of 0.340 cm and an SD of 0.140 cm (that's a very BIG standard deviation). Now the daily X-bar and S control charts look like those shown on the following page.

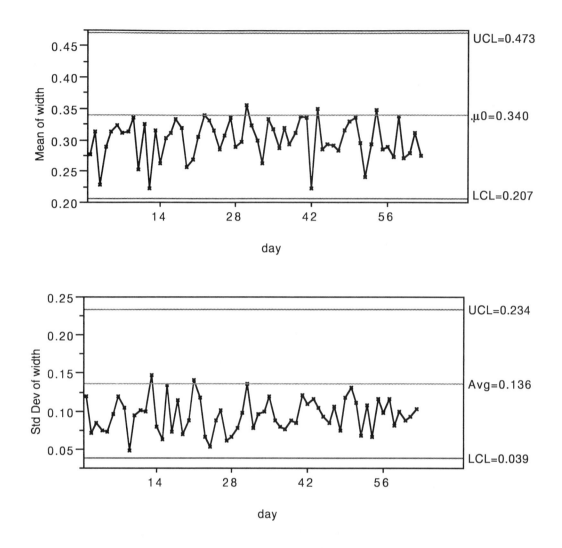

With these different specifications for the mean and SD, the process is capable and also in control if we use our ± 3 SE(mean) rule.

Suppose, however, that we use a different rule for deciding whether the process is capable. True, the means are all inside the control limits, but they consistently fall below the target specified value. It appears that the process mean is below 0.340 cm, but not so much to carry the means below the control limits.

Other tests based on control charts use other methods to determine if a process is behaving properly. One such test, number 2 in JMP's list, claims that the process is not capable if nine consecutive means fall on the same side of the target mean. Checking test box 2 in the JMP control chart dialog box gives us the chart shown at the top of the next page.

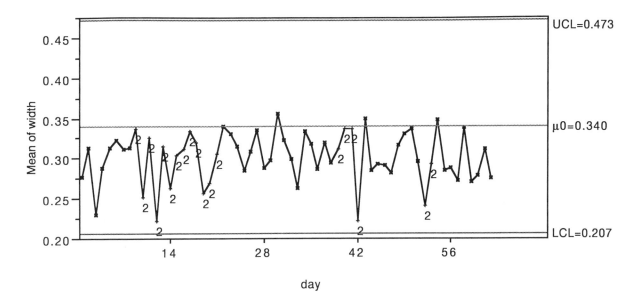

JMP flags with the "2" labels days where nine or more consecutive means have fallen on the same side of the target. In this case, the test would indicate that the process was not capable, and that the process mean was smaller than the target (as we know from our previous work on this example).

A reasonable question is "Why 9 days? Why not 4 or 12?" Presumably we would not want a test that flagged the process as not capable if the means were on the same side of the chart 2 days in a row. That would sound too many "false alarms." With the 9 consecutive days rule, *what are the chances of a false alarm?* The calculations are similar to those in our previous discussion of "miracles."

Assuming that the target mean is correct, the chance of a sample mean lying below the target on a randomly chosen day is $1/2$, and the same for the chance of lying above the target. Now assume that the results from each day have no effect on each other; that is, that the results are independent as in flipping a fair coin. The temptation is to say that the chance of a false alarm is the same as the chance of getting either nine consecutive heads or nine consecutive tails when tossing a coin. That probability is

Pr(HHHHHHHHH *OR* TTTTTTTTT)

$$= \text{Pr(HHHHHHHHH)} + \text{Pr(TTTTTTTTT)}$$

$$= (.5)(.5)(.5)(.5)(.5)(.5)(.5)(.5)(.5) + (.5)(.5)(.5)(.5)(.5)(.5)(.5)(.5)(.5)$$

$$= .5^9 + .5^9 = .0039$$

There are two particular concerns with this calculation. The first is a reminder about *assumptions*. We assumed that the probability of a sample mean's being below the target mean is $1/2$ throughout this period. That assumes that the target mean is also the target median, a reasonable assumption if the distribution of the data is symmetric (it is). Also, we made the assumption that the results from one day to the next are independent. What if there were trends in the seam widths? For example, suppose that the seams were low for five days, then high for five days, then low for five days, and so forth. Such cycles would imply a lack of independence and indicate that our probability calculation was off target. For this example, we can't see any evident trends, so the assumption of independence seems plausible.

The second concern is more important and a bit less obvious. We started off by asking the wrong question! We computed the probability of "nine in a row" for a given set of nine days. But what is the probability of finding "nine in a row" somewhere in our 62 day period? There are many nine day periods within 62 days (54 to be precise), and any one of these could have produced the "nine in a row."

Actually calculating the probability that we want is pretty hard in this case because the nine day periods overlap — they're not independent. Rather than think about this one for too long, we simply wrote a small computer program to *simulate* the process. Relying on our assumptions, it simulates tossing a coin 62 times and counts whether we got "nine in a row" (a run of nine or more heads or tails). In 1000 such sequences of 62 tosses, there were 87 false alarms so that the chance of at least one false alarm in a 62 day period is about 0.087, nearly 10%. That's quite a bit higher than 0.0039.

Analysis of Production of Computer Chips

CompChip.jmp

A manufacturer of computer chips was concerned about maintaining proper thickness of coating on the chips. Prior experience with the process when it has functioned according to specifications indicates that the mean thickness should be 250 with standard deviation of 1.5 units when the process is functioning properly.

Is the production output meeting these standards? Is the process under control?

To monitor the production process, the manufacturer measured the thickness of 12 chips each day chosen at random from the production line on each of 40 consecutive days. Using the notions developed in the previous examples, the control limits are

$$250 \pm 3(1.5/\sqrt{12}) = 250 \pm 1.3.$$

The marginal histogram appears somewhat normal with no evident skewness, but there are quite a few outliers.

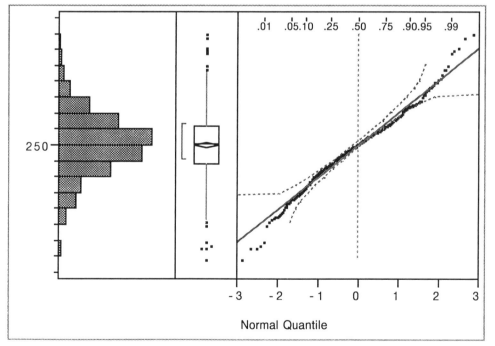

The center line for the X-bar chart is the midpoint of the control range, 250 units, and the upper and lower limits are those set by the specifications. Two daily averages are near the upper limit and one is clearly below the lower limit. Although most of the means are within the control limits, a distinct pattern is apparent. A slight upward drift appears until day 18, and then the daily averages begin to fluctuate in a much more pronounced fashion.

The S chart clarifies the trouble. Variability increases slowly until day 22 but stays within specifications. Then it rises and fluctuates markedly.

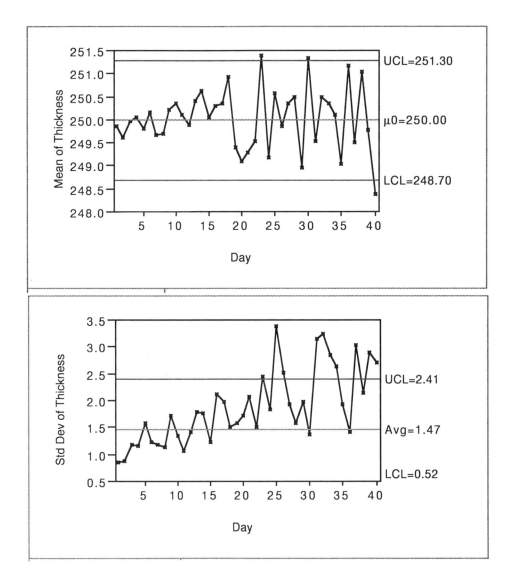

The next plot compares the data prior to and on day 20 to the data after day 20. The earlier data are less variable.

Thickness by After Day 20?

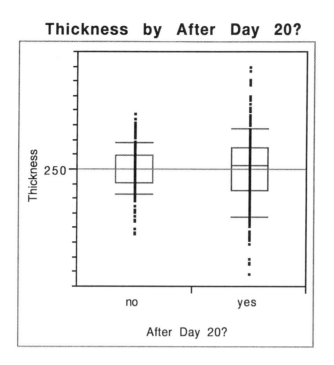

Means and Std Deviations

Level	Number	Mean	Std Dev	Std Err Mean
no	240	250.041	1.472	0.0950
yes	240	250.029	2.469	0.1594

The causes of the slow upward drift in both charts in the first 20 days, and of the increase in variability in the last 20 days, should be explored. It is instructive in this example to do separate analyses of the first 20 days and the second 20 days. Side-by-side comparison plots clearly show the difference in variability between the two halves of the data set.

A manufacturer of computer chips was concerned about maintaining proper thickness of coating on the chips. The specifications call for an average of 250 units, with a standard deviation of 1.5 units. Is the production output meeting these standards?

The process began this period in control, with both the mean and the standard deviation within limits. Gradually, though, the process went out of control. The means slowly grew until about day 20, then suddenly decreased. The standard deviation crept upward prior to day 20 and then became very erratic and frequently exceeded the control limits.

For this example, a good question to ask is why the process was allowed to continue running for so long after going outside the control limits. Perhaps no one was watching.

A Reminder:

When working with control charts, the limits must be determined based on information about the process when it is in control. Otherwise, other sources of variation, such as trends, will inflate the baseline measure of variation and produce wide control limits that are unable to detect problems in the process. The default limits that JMP assigns to a control chart use all of the data and assume that the process is in control.

Class 5.   Confidence Intervals

We all sense that large samples are more informative than small ones, because of something vaguely called the "law of averages." This class considers how to use the information in a sample to make a claim about some population feature. The normal distribution plays a key role.

The standard error of the sample average measures the precision of the average and is related to how close one might expect the average to approximate the unknown true process mean. A confidence interval allows us to quantify just how close we expect the sample average to be to the process mean.

After discussing confidence intervals, we introduce several issues in sample survey design. Often, if we are dissatisfied with the width of the confidence interval and want to make it smaller, we have little choice but to reconsider the sample — larger samples produce shorter intervals. Larger samples also cost more and may not be the most efficient way to gather information.

Topics

    Confidence versus precision; confidence coefficient

    Checking assumptions

Examples

    Interval estimates of the process mean (continued)

    Purchases of consumer goods

Key Application

Making an informative statement about a process mean. When the process is found to be in control, it makes sense to talk about the overall process mean. This process mean conveys information about the typical state of the process, and so it is desirable to make the most informative statement that we can about its value. First it is important to realize that the true process mean is unknown (technically we call it a parameter), and the best that we can do is to estimate it from a sample of observations (using a statistic such as the sample mean).

Consider now a scenario in which you and a co-worker have taken sample measurements. Being diligent, you have taken 100 observations on the process ($n =$

100), whereas your less diligent co-worker has taken just 10 ($n = 10$). You will both get sample means: if this is all that you report to your boss, then it is impossible to tell that your estimate (based on $n = 100$) is somehow "better" than your co-worker's. The value of the extra time and money spent on your more extensive sample is lost if all you do is report your best guess, the sample mean.

Definition

Confidence interval for the mean. A range of feasible values for an unknown population/process mean together with a confidence coefficient conveying the confidence that one has that the true mean actually lies in the interval.

Confidence coefficient. This is another term for the probability associated with a confidence interval. For example, the confidence coefficient of a 95% confidence interval is 0.95.

Concepts

Confidence interval. A valuable way of reporting your answer, one that summarizes and exhausts almost all the useful information in the sample (and furthermore, in the above example, reflects the extra effort you have put in above that of your co-worker).

A confidence interval conveys two important pieces of information. First, it shows an entire range of feasible values for the true but unknown process mean rather than just a best guess. Second, the interval is associated with a degree of confidence that reflects your belief that the true but actually unknown process mean lies in your interval. You can see that a confidence interval statement is a far more sophisticated concept than just reporting a best guess.

Think of a confidence interval as a two-level statement, the first being the range of feasible values, the second being a statement that elaborates the first statement in the sense that it tells you how much confidence we have in the first statement. To reiterate, a confidence interval is not only a way of providing an answer (the range of feasible values) but also a way of telling someone how likely your answer is to be correct (the confidence coefficient).

It is quite remarkable that we can use data not only to give us answers but also to tell us how good or valuable the answer is likely to be. It is this "meta" level statement, one that conveys that accuracy of your results, that really separates statistical thinking from other forms of quantitative analysis. It is not always an easy concept to live with, and certainly it is not as widely used as one might expect. Of course, anyone can make a guess about anything, but it is quite unsettling when the quality of your guess is evaluated statistically via a confidence coefficient and is found to be lacking.

An informal way of understanding confidence intervals is given by combining the following set of relations that ties together all that we have learned so far:

1. (Empirical rule) Providing the data is bell shaped and symmetric, the empirical rule tells us that 95% of the data points will lie within ±2 SD from the true mean.

2. (Central limit theorem) The central limit theorem tells us that the sample mean has an approximate normal distribution (bell-shaped and symmetric). Therefore if we apply the empirical rule to the sample mean itself we get:

95% of the time the sample mean $\overline{X}$ lies within 2 SEs of μ.

We have gone from SD to SE because statement 1 is about the data whose dispersion is measured by the SD, whereas statement 2 is about the sample mean whose dispersion is measured by SE.

3. (Inversion) If 95% of the time the sample mean is within ±2 SE from the true but unknown population mean, then 95% of the time the true but unknown population mean must be within ±2 SEs from $\overline{X}$. This means that the interval

$$\overline{X} \pm 2\frac{s}{\sqrt{n}} \quad ,$$

where

$$SE = \frac{s}{\sqrt{n}} \quad ,$$

will give us the range of feasible values that we sought. The 2 is in there because we are doing a 95% confidence interval. If you wanted a 90% CI, then replace 2 by 1.65. Tables abound that give you other levels of confidence and longer or shorter intervals.

Heuristics

Plus or minus two standard errors. An approximate 95% confidence interval for the population mean is given by the sample mean plus or minus twice its standard error.

Potential Confuser

The $\sqrt{n}$ factor again. Always remember that the standard error (SE) of the mean has the $\sqrt{n}$ divisor. The standard error rewards you for hard work because a bigger sample size n

leads to a smaller SE and consequently a smaller confidence interval. Smaller confidence intervals are good because they give us a tighter range of feasible values.

Interval Estimates of the Process Mean (Continued)

ShaftXtr.jmp

Engineering is considering a redesign of the engines produced at our assembly plant. The diameter of the typical shaft is crucial in this revision. If the process mean is less than 812 mils, expensive new bearings must be designed for the engine.

What is our best estimate of the process mean, and can we quantify our uncertainty?

We return one last time to the data used in Class 4. Recall that the sample data give the diameters of 400 shafts sampled from our production process. In our previous work with these data, we sought to determine if this process was capable and in control. Now we would like to determine what we can say about the steady-state process.

In particular, the engineers are most interested in the average *process* diameter — the mean of *all* of the shafts produced by the process, not simply the mean diameter of a sample of 100 or 400 shafts. Here is the problem. Were we able to measure the diameter of *every* shaft produced by this process, we would know the distribution of the process. If we drew the histogram of this extremely large collection of diameters, it might resemble the following very smooth curve since the histogram bins would be quite small.

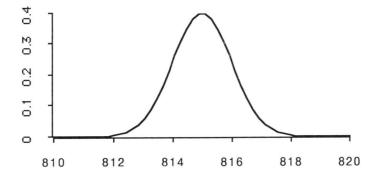

However, we do not observe this "population" or process histogram and must instead rely upon a sample. The distribution of the sample resembles the distribution of the process, but it is not the same. In fact, if we were to repeat the sampling process, we would get a different sample, with a different histogram and different summary statistics.

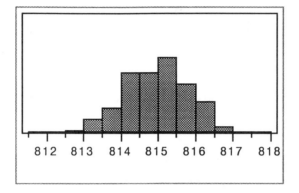

Since we cannot observe the process distribution, we need to determine what we can say about its features, such as its mean, using only a sample. Recall our notation for sample and population values. Greek letters typically describe features of the process, and Latin counterparts denote the sample analogs.

	Population Feature	Sample Characteristic
Mean	μ	$\bar{X}$
Standard deviation (SD)	σ	s
Variance	σ^2	s^2

Using this common notation, our problem is to make some statement about the value of μ, the process mean, using only characteristics of the sample, such as the sample mean, $\bar{X}$, or the sample standard deviation, s.

The histogram of the 400 shaft diameters is reproduced below. Since the process has been found to be in control, we can combine the data into a single batch rather than work with daily or weekly summaries. The data look quite normally distributed.

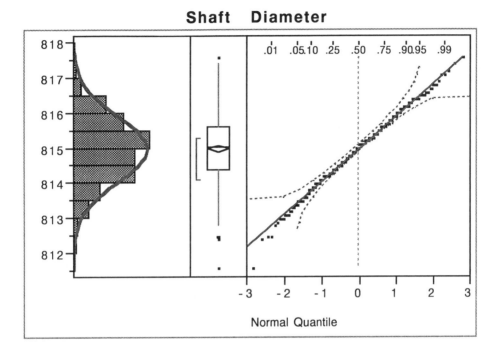

The ideas that combine the empirical rule and the standard error of the sample mean lead to a solution of this problem. The resulting interval is known as a confidence interval for the process (or population) mean μ. From our work with control charts, we know that the interval

$$\mu \pm 2 \, \mathrm{SE}(\overline{X}) = \mu \pm 2 \, \frac{\sigma}{\sqrt{n}}$$

contains the sample mean $\overline{X}$ about 95% of the time. Using a bit more notation, we can write this property more formally as

$$\Pr \{\mu - 2 \, \mathrm{SE}(\overline{X}) \le \overline{X} \le \mu + 2 \, \mathrm{SE}(\overline{X})\} \approx 0.95 \; .$$

The interesting idea is to "invert" this statement into one that makes a claim about where the true mean lies given values for SE and the sample mean. In particular, by rearranging the terms, we obtain

$$\Pr \{\overline{X} - 2 \, \mathrm{SE}(\overline{X}) \le \mu \le \overline{X} + 2 \, \mathrm{SE}(\overline{X})\} \approx 0.95 \; .$$

The resulting interval, $[\bar{X} - 2\,SE(\bar{X}),\ \bar{X} + 2\,SE(\bar{X})]$ is known as a 95% confidence interval for the unknown population mean μ. (In fact, one uses a value slightly different from 2 to get the interval to be precisely 95%.) The JMP summary output gives this interval as well as the value of the standard error

$$\text{sample } SE(\bar{X}) = s/\sqrt{n} = 0.93/\sqrt{400} = 0.0465.$$

The diamond shown by default in boxplots is this confidence interval for the mean.

Moments

Mean	814.99	
Std Dev	0.93	
Std Err Mean	0.0465	<---- $SE(\bar{X})$
upper 95% Mean	815.1	<---- lower CI endpt
lower 95% Mean	814.9	<---- upper CI endpt
N	400	

The use of a confidence interval to make claims about the unobserved process mean implies that we *accept a certain level of risk.* The 95% interval for the process mean diameter is [814.90, 815.08]. We can be pretty sure that the process mean lies within this interval, though we may be wrong. For example, the process mean might be 814.8; this result is unlikely, but it could occur. The only confidence interval that is 100% accurate is not very useful, namely the interval $[-\infty, +\infty]$ that allows any possible value.

Perhaps we think that this confidence interval is too wide. Maybe our design tolerances require a more narrow interval. We have two ways to get something shorter than this interval:

       (1) measure more shafts to have a larger sample; or

       (2) accept more risk of being wrong.

With a 95% interval, we are taking a 100% – 95% = 5% risk of being wrong with our claimed range allowed for the process mean. The value 0.95 is known as the *level of confidence,* or the *confidence coefficient* of the interval.

To illustrate, if we look at the confidence intervals implied by the five shafts measured each day, notice that the interval for day 24 does not include the value, 815, which we believe using all of the data is the process mean. (Use the *Fit Y by X* command to get this plot, and then add the means diamonds to the resulting display using the Display button below the resulting plot. In order to fit on the page, the plot shows just the data for the first 30 days.)

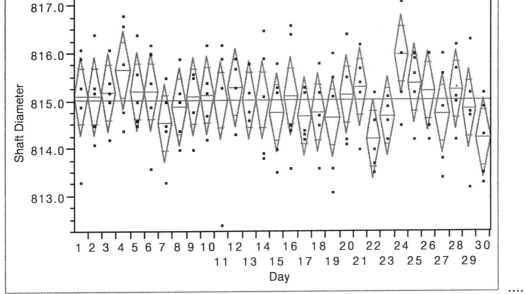

Given this risk for making an error, might the process mean be as low as the crucial 812 mils? Not likely. For example, we can see what would happen if we used a less standard 99.73% confidence interval $[\bar{X} \pm 3\,SE]$ – one that contains the process mean with probability 0.9973. Using the empirical rule, the interval would be about

$$[815 \pm 3\,(0.0465)] = [815 - 0.14,\ 815 + 0.14]\,.$$ **±3 SE**

We are 99.7% sure that 812 is not the process mean. Even if we were to use the almost certain interval $[\bar{X} \pm 4\,SE]$, 812 would not lie within the confidence interval,

$$[815 \pm 4(0.0465)] = [815 - 0.19,\ 815 + 0.19]\,.$$ **±4 SE**

Engineering is considering a redesign of the engines produced at our assembly plant. The diameter of the typical shaft is crucial in this revision. If the process mean is less than 812 mils, new and expensive special bearings must be designed. What is our best estimate of the process mean, and can we quantify our uncertainty?

The 95% interval for the process mean μ is [814.90, 815.08]. This interval is far from the 812 design threshold, and it seems clear that the special bearings will not be needed.

Review of Assumptions

As we start to make use of more statistical methods, we need to keep track of the underlying assumptions needed for the validity of the results. Those that apply here in the case of the confidence interval for the mean will show up again and again. The assumptions made by the standard interval (formally known as the t-interval) are that the observations

(1) are independent of each other (i.e., there is no evident trend),

(2) arise from a normal population (or at least close to normal), and

(3) have constant variance.

All three seem reasonable in the context of this example. The second assumption is less crucial than the others because of the central limit theorem. If skewness is an issue, consider the p-value computed using ranks and reported in the output of the testing procedure discussed next.

Testing: An Alternative Approach

One often sees problems of inferring population features from a sample approached by another method known as a hypothesis test. The basic idea of these tests is to measure how far the observed mean (or other statistic) lies from a conjectured population value. The relevant "distance" to use is to count the number of standard errors that separate the statistic from the conjectured, or hypothesized, value. In the example just completed, the conjectured value for the population mean 812 is

$$t = \frac{814.99 - 812}{.0465} \approx 64.3$$

standard errors below the observed sample average. This ratio, which counts the number of standard errors separating the observed statistic and a hypothesized population value, is known as a *t*-ratio or a *t*-statistic. The empirical rule implies that deviations of this size simply don't happen, and thus 812 is highly unlikely to be the population value.

Using the testing option provided at the top of the histogram display, JMP computes the probability of this sort of deviation to be zero. The probability of seeing a sample average as large as that we have observed is zero if indeed the process mean were 812. Thus we conclude that the process mean is not 812 and must be larger.

Test Mean = value

	Hypothesized Value	812
	Actual Estimate	814.992

	t Test	Signed-Rank	
Test Statistic	64.349	40098.5	<--- # of SEs from hyp value
Prob > ltl	0.000	0.000	
Prob > t	0.000	0.000	
Prob < t	1.000	1.000	

We will return to the use of tests similar to these in Class 7.

Purchases of Consumer Goods

CompPur.jmp

A manufacturer of consumer electronics would like to know how many households intend to purchase a computer during the next year. A survey has collected responses from 100 households. Management is hoping that the proportion is at least 25% in order to justify sales projections.

Based on this sample, should management start revising those estimates?

The notion of a confidence interval also applies to proportions. In fact, reported poll results such as those that accompany most elections or important political debates include confidence intervals, usually disguised by a phrase such as "survey results are accurate to within plus or minus 3%."

The initial histogram of the response is a categorical variable (categorical variables indicate group membership — here coded literally as "Yes" and "No" — as opposed to numerical values). The number of responses coded "No" suggests that the proportion of households in this sample that intend to purchase a computer is smaller than hoped. Only 14 of the 100 surveyed households indicate that they plan to purchase a computer in the coming year.

Intend to Purchase

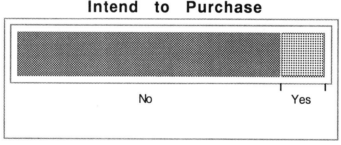

Frequencies

Level	Count	Probability	Cum Prob
No	86	0.86000	0.86000
Yes	14	0.14000	1.00000
Total	100		

Is this small proportion a fluke? That is, if we went out and surveyed 100 more households, are we likely to see a very different sample proportion — perhaps one that indicates that the sales projections are reasonable?

A confidence interval for the population proportion is often used to assess the precision of a sample estimate. Our sample has 14% who indicate that they intend to purchase a computer in the coming year. How far might this sample proportion be from the population proportion — the proportion we would observe had we the time and money to survey all households?

To get JMP to report the 95% interval, we need to have a numerical variable. We cannot use the variable coded as "yes" and "no," no matter how much more logical it might seem. Instead, we have to code the values as numbers, with 1 for yes and 0 for no. A variable coded in this way is known as a "dummy variable." With this 0/1 coding, the sample average is the desired proportion.

The output (unattractive as it is) shows the 95% interval for μ as a superimposed diamond in the quantile boxplot (rather than the outlier boxplot). The precise endpoints of the interval appear with the summary statistics marked below.

Intend?

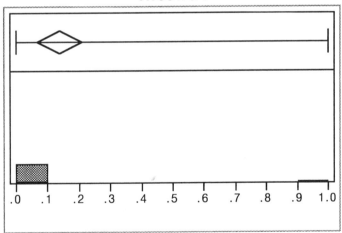

Moments

Mean	0.1400	
Std Dev	0.3487	
Std Err Mean	0.0349	
upper 95% Mean	**0.2092**	<--- interval
lower 95% Mean	**0.0708**	<--- endpoints
N	100	

A manufacturer of consumer electronics would like to know how many households intend to purchase a computer during the next year. A survey has collected responses from 100 households. Management is hoping that the proportion is at least 25% in order to justify sales projections.

Based on this sample, should management start revising those estimates?

The confidence interval for the population proportion suggests that management better revise the estimates. The sample proportion is close to 15%, and the 95% interval excludes the critical value 0.25, suggesting that this proportion is unrealistically large.

Some Additional Comments

(1) While traditional, there is nothing sacred about the choice of a 95% level of confidence. We can use a smaller or larger value, and adjust the associated multiplier in the expression for the interval. To get an interval that is more likely to contain μ — one with a higher confidence coefficient — we have to increase the multiplier and thus get a longer interval. Shrinking the level of confidence leads to a smaller multiplier and shorter interval.

(2) Just because consumers indicate that they intend to purchase an item in the coming year is often not indicative of their later behavior. The marketing research literature is full of papers on the distinction between one's intent to purchase and the actual purchase.

(3) We know that 0.25 lies outside the 95% interval, so this is an unlikely value for the population proportion. To be within the interval, 0.25 must be within 2 SEs of the sample proportion 0.14. It is not. From the output on the previous page, we have

$$\frac{.25 - .14}{.0349} \approx 3.15 .$$

That is, the hoped for population proportion lies 3.15 standard errors above the observed sample proportion and hence is far outside the 95% interval (and is also outside the 99.73% interval $[\bar{X} \pm 3 \text{ SE}]$).

Class 6. Sampling

This class introduces the basic issues concerned with collecting information. The problem of making a valid inference about a population based on information obtained in a sample will be the main focus. For this inference to be valid, the sample needs to be representative. Though this sounds like common sense, subtle biases often creep in when sampling is done. When this is the case, the inference may be very misleading. We will discuss some of these biases and explain sampling methods designed to avoid bias.

A key idea is the concept of a *random sample*. The planned introduction of randomness into the sample allows valid and reliable inferences to be made. Naturally, this randomness introduces some uncertainty, but the measures of variability introduced in previous classes provide a means for quantifying this uncertainty.

Topics

 Simple random sample

 Why the sample must be representative

 Questionnaire design and sample validity

 Inference about the population

 Random sampling schemes that ensure a representative sample.

 Sample biases

 Non-response and missing data, confounding, length biased samples

Example

 Internet use surveys

 Hotel satisfaction survey

Key Application

Obtaining reliable information cost effectively. Since the inferences that we have been making are based on data, it is clear that if something is wrong with the data then something is going to be wrong with the inference. Recall that a core component of statistics is to make statements about a population of interest based on a sample from that population. A common thing that goes wrong is that the sample we have been talking about is not in fact representative of the population.

Imagine, for example, that you wished to make inference about starting salaries of MBA graduates and you sampled only Wharton MBAs. Not a good start. It is not that Wharton MBA's are not part of the population. Rather, they are simply not representative of the population at large. This is an example of what is called *sampling bias*. Statistical approaches to quantitative analysis provide for a way, known as *simple random sampling*, of collecting data that ensures that the data are representative of the population.

Sampling bias arises in a variety of ways, some of which are illustrated in the two examples of this class. Among the many sources of bias, we can list

(1) *Self-selection*. Rather that find a true random sample, it is often easier to collect responses from those who send them back or are willing to talk on the phone than to try to get each initially selected respondent to participate. For example, someone might distribute a questionnaire to all of the students in a school and just use the responses of those who return the form. You might see the result called a survey since, say, only 20% return the forms, but this sample is not likely to be representative.

(2) *Question formulation*. Often the wording of a question can have a profound impact on the way that the respondent answers. By adding either favorable or unfavorable context information, the questioner can affect the response. Here is an extreme example. The question "Would you be interested in purchasing this large, sport vehicle that will make you safe in an accident?" is going to get a very different reaction to the same vehicle than a question like "Would you be interested in purchasing this large, sport vehicle that burns a lot of gas and pollutes the environment?" In other cases, the respondent may not understand the question, or misinterprets what is being asked.

(3) *Interviewer characteristics*. Recent studies at the University of Michigan have found that the perceived race of the interviewer will affect respondents' answers even in telephone surveys. The reactions of white respondents, for example, depended on whether they thought that the interviewer was also white. Similar effects applied for other races as well, with the size of the effect depending on the nature of the question.

(4) *Question sensitivity*. Do you use drugs? It's hard to believe that you can completely trust someone's answer that would amount to them admitting the commission of a crime. Special techniques, including one known as randomized response, have been developed to obtain good answers to sensitive questions. The same effects show up in political polls as well. In the 1992 British election, polling suggested that Kinnock from the Labor Party would win, but the election went to the Conservative, John Major. The polling error was attributed to "shy Tories," voters who were embarrassed to admit that they were voting for the Conservative Party. In the more recent 1997 election that saw Major and the Conservatives lose to the Labor candidate Blair, pollers attempted to correct for this effect. Such adjustments based on past behavior are tricky to use. In this case, the adjustments went too far and overestimated the Conservative share.

Overview

Comparison to a census. Samples possess a number of advantages compared to a census. Although it is tempting in this age of computers and high-speed networks to try to collect complete information on the entire population of interest, a sample is often better. Keep in mind the following points:

A. Completing a census is relatively time-consuming.

B. Collecting a census requires many more personnel than a sample does.

C. Because of these needs, a census is often many times more expensive than a sample.

In the end it may be better to get a small amount of high-quality information than a large amount of low-quality information. Indeed, many statisticians at the U.S. Bureau of the Census believe that well-done surveys give a more accurate picture of the U.S. population than a less-careful census.

Inferential methods such as confidence intervals rely on a sample that has been drawn from a population in order to estimate a population characteristic. For example, what proportion of all taxpayers submit correct returns? The population is the collection of all taxpayers, and the characteristic of interest is the accuracy of the submitted forms. Similarly, what is the average savings rate of American households? The population consists of all American households (try to define this!), and the attribute is the average savings rate.

Several important questions. Several issues arise in virtually every survey. Whenever designing a survey or using the results of a survey, consider the following questions:

1. What is the target population? Does it differ from the population actually sampled?

2. Which units from this population should be sampled? That is, what is the sampling unit?

3. How many observations should be sampled? With too few, you will not have enough data to make accurate inference. With too many, it is just overkill and a waste of time and resources.

4. How will you deal with nonresponse? Are responses that are missing similar to those that respond?

5. Have any of several possible factors produced a biased sample?

Definitions

Simple random sample. A subset of the population in which all items are equally likely and independently chosen, abbreviated as SRS.

Biased sample. A sample that is systematically unrepresentative of the population (sampling:bias).

Census. A collection representing the entire population.

Concepts

Simple random sample. An SRS is a sample in which all units of the population are equally likely to be chosen and in which units are sampled independently. You can obtain an SRS by labeling every single unit in the population with a number and then drawing (on a computer) a random sample without replacement from the list of numbers. Actually, though it is very easy to draw a random sample once you have the population defined and listed, the really hard thing to do is to get the list of all the units in the population. Often, for instance, the population changes during the enumeration process. Take the Internet, for example. Samples that aim to draw inferences about who uses the Internet are notoriously biased partly because the entity is so dynamic that it is impossible to list a population.

Heuristics

How many people do you need to sample in order to obtain a 95% CI for a proportion that has a specified margin of error? Here, "margin of error" is half the width of a 95% confidence interval. Answer: $1/(\text{margin of error})^2$.

Internet Use Surveys

What sort of customers will see the ads that my company is thinking of putting on the Internet?

One area that has recently attracted a lot of attention is the size and demographic profile of Internet users. The relevance to commerce is obvious — does a new retirement community in Arizona really need to set up a Web site to attract new business? Will any of its potential customers see the ads?

Many different surveys have been undertaken to get a handle on such questions. Here we will contrast two such surveys, one from Georgia Tech and the second gathered by the A. C. Nielson Company. The first is a user survey from Georgia Tech's Graphics, Visualization & Usability (GVU) Center. The data are available on-line from the Internet at the URL

http://www.cc.gatech.edu/gvu/user_surveys/

This survey has been repeated every six months since January 1994, but we will focus on the 5th survey, conducted in April 1996, which collected approximately 11,700 respondents.

When judging the value of this survey, two key aspects need to be recognized:

- first, only a subset of all users have the opportunity to take the survey — those that see it advertised;

- second, of those that see it advertised, participants self-select into the survey.

These two components set the stage for potential biases in the respondent sample when compared to all users of the Internet. Consequently, a key problem with this sort of survey is that it is very hard to extrapolate the results to the population of interest with any sort of confidence. If a large proportion of the sample consists of college students, does it mean that most users of the Web are college students? Or, is it just that college students have more access and time to surf the Web and fill out on-line questionnaires?

A second survey of the Internet was conducted jointly by CommerceNet/Nielsen Research. They employed a very different sampling mechanism. The respondents were chosen using a probability sample of people living in households with telephones in the United States and Canada. A probability sample means that each unit of the population has some known probability of being included in the sample. Even though there is always the possibility of self-selection into the survey (people who hang up the phone at the hint of a survey question do not get into the survey), considerable efforts were made to obtain an accurate sample, with up to eight attempts made to reach a selected household.

How "valuable" is the information in each of the surveys? One surrogate measure of this is just how much each organization charges for the data it obtains. All data from the GVU survey are available for free. On the other hand, the CommerceNet/Nielsen survey can be purchased for $5000. Though it's tempting to claim that "You get what you pay for," this reaction is jumping the gun a bit. In particular, the value of the data depends on the question you are trying to answer. For some basic demographics such as gender ratios, the two surveys agree quite well, whereas on other topics such as income of users they differ substantially.

Furthermore, just because you pay for data does not necessarily make that data better. The CommerceNet/Nielsen survey had a few biases of its own. To start with, it only involved individuals with a telephone. While this may represent 95% of the U.S. population, it does of course miss the other 5%. If your question of interest concerns issues of equal access to information and educational resources regardless of socio-economic status, then this survey may not be as informative as you had hoped. People without access to a telephone are precisely some of the people on whom you would like to get data. Other claimed biases in this survey include an over-representation of highly educated individuals. More details about these concerns appear on the Web itself on a page prepared by the Project 2000 group at

http://www2000.ogsm.vanderbilt.edu/surveys/cn.questions.html

To compare the data between the surveys, the table on the next page shows the household income distribution (in thousands of U.S. dollars) of the respondents according to the two surveys. For completeness, the table includes U.S. Census data from 1990. Comparisons are very difficult because the sampling units are different. The Census Bureau samples households, whereas the Nielsen and GVU surveys sample individuals.

Income bracket	Census	Nielsen	GVU
20-	33	19	11
20 – 39.9	32	32	20
40 – 59.9	19	24	20
60+	16	24	49

The numbers look very different between the census and the surveys; you have to be careful to understand just exactly what they are measuring. The 33 in the Census column for the under $20,000 incomes says that 33% of U.S. households have incomes less than $20,000. The 19 in the Nielsen column says that approximately 19% of individuals are in households with incomes under $20,000. The 11 in the GVU column says that 11% of the individuals who filled out the GVU survey live in households with incomes below $20,000. Even though all three numbers are different, each of them answers a different question, so they are not necessarily contradictory!

The message here is that you have to think very carefully about just exactly what question you are asking before you find data to answer it. If you are in the business of selling information, then the quality and credibility of that information become paramount. To the people in these businesses, "random and representative sampling" is a core component in the quality of their final product.

Hotel Satisfaction Survey

Survey1.jmp and Survey2.jmp

A hotel chain in the Southeast wishes to construct an in-depth profile of its customer base. Management is interested in socioeconomic characteristics of the guests as well as the impact of advertising campaigns. Of particular interest is learning how many guests plan to return to hotels in this chain.

Currently the only information collected on the clientele is taken from voluntary customer satisfaction surveys that are left in hotel rooms; only 10% of guests complete the forms. Management is of the opinion that these surveys do not genuinely reflect customer feelings because only very angry or very happy customers fill them out.

How can the chain use a survey to learn more about its guests and their future travel plans?

In order to collect more extensive information about its guests, the management of the hotel chain initiates a survey. Two questions immediately arise:

Question 1.   Who should be interviewed?

Question 2.   How large a sample should be taken?

To answer Question 1, the population for inference must be identified so that a representative sample can be collected. It is decided that the population will be "all primary customers." "Primary" is defined as the person who signs the register and is ultimately responsible for payment. The sample needs to be a representative cross section of the primary customers.

To answer Question 2, a main attribute of interest (sometimes called the "survey variable") is identified: what proportion of primary customers intend to use the hotel chain again within the next year? This has been chosen as the critical metric by which to evaluate overall customer satisfaction. Since this will be estimated, a confidence interval is needed. A level of precision, ±3%, at 95% confidence is adopted, which suggests a sample size of slightly more than 1100.

Here is a "rule of thumb" you can use to approximate the required sample size. As long as the unknown proportion lies in the range $1/4$ to $3/4$ and you are using a 95% interval, use the following rule:

$$\text{sample size} = \frac{1}{(\text{margin of error})^2} \ .$$

For this example, the margin or error in this example is 0.03, so that we have

$$\text{sample size} = \frac{1}{0.03^2} = \frac{1}{0.0009} = 1111.$$

Since the chain has about this many guests on any day during the travel season, it was decided to interview every primary guest present on June 15, 1994. Those guests who were not interviewed at the hotel were contacted by telephone. It was possible to contact 97% of those present, an exceptionally high response rate.

Whenever nonresponse occurs in a survey, it is important to understand whether the nonrespondents differ from the respondents in terms of the survey variable. This issue becomes more important as the proportion of nonresponse in the survey increases. With a response rate of 97%, the results of this survey are likely to be reliable, though you might want to consider the implications of a "worst-case" analysis: suppose everyone who did not response would say either "yes" or "no" to the key question of a return visit.

Summary statistics on three variables collected in the survey follow: length of stay, sex and whether or not the respondent intended to revisit within the next year. The length-of-stay variable can take on any integer value, and we shall treat it as continuous. From the output on the next page, we can see that about 63% of the guests in the chain on the surveyed day in June indicated that they planned to return within the next year. The second histogram shows that most of the "primary" guests were men.

Will   Return?

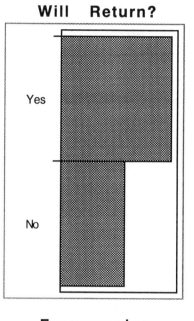

Frequencies

Level	Count	Probability	Cum Prob
No	416	0.37011	0.37011
Yes	708	0.62989	1.00000
Total	1124		

Sex

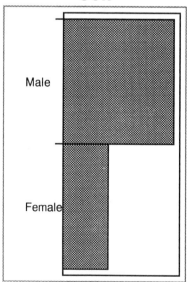

Frequencies

Sex	Count	Probability	Cum Prob
Female	331	0.294	0.294
Male	793	0.705	1.000
Total	1124		

The length-of-stay data are heavily skewed, with a few staying for a visit of a month or longer.

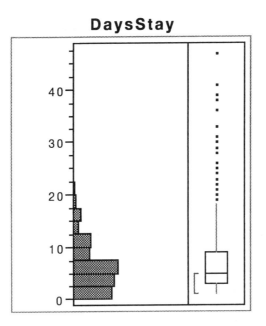

DaysStay

Quantiles

maximum	100.0%	47
quartile	75.0%	9
median	50.0%	5
quartile	25.0%	3
minimum	0.0%	1

Moments

Mean	6.701
Std Dev	5.614
Std Err Mean	0.167
upper 95% Mean	7.030
lower 95% Mean	6.372
N	1124

A simple crosstabulation indicates that there is little or no relationship between the sex of the guest and the issue of a return visit. The proportion of women saying that they plan to return to the hotel chain in the next year is

$$\text{proportion of women indicating plans to return} = \frac{201}{331} \approx 0.61,$$

whereas

$$\text{proportion of men indicating plans to return} = \frac{507}{793} \approx 0.64 .$$

(JMP produces this table when you use the *Fit Y by X* command of the *Analyze* menu, and the data are nominal such as these. The accompanying figure is not shown.)

Crosstabs

Will Return? Count Total %	Sex Female	Male		
No	130	286		416
	11.57	25.44		37.01
Yes	201	507		708
	17.88	45.11		62.99
Total	331	793		1124
	29.45	70.55		

The various probabilities reported with this table confirm our intuitive impression: the two factors are evidently independent of one another.

Test	ChiSquare	Prob>ChiSq
Likelihood Ratio	1.027	0.3109
Pearson	1.032	0.3097

Fisher's	Exact	TestProb
Left		0.8606
Right		0.1715
2-Tail		0.3104

In order to build a comparable table for the relationship of the duration of stay and the question of future plans, we have built a derived variable, labeled *LongStay?*. *LongStay?* is coded "yes" if the duration of the stay is six or more days. This factor appears to be quite highly related to the variable of interest. Of the 591 whose visit lasted less than six days, the chances of indicating that they will return is relatively small,

$$\text{proportion of those whose visit was short who plan to return} = \frac{270}{591} \approx 0.46,$$

whereas for those who stayed for six or more days, the proportion is almost twice as high:

$$\text{proportion of those whose visit was long who plan to return} = \frac{438}{533} \approx 0.82 \, .$$

Crosstabs

Will Return? Count Total %	Long Stay? No	Yes		
No	321	95		416
	28.56	8.45		37.01
Yes	270	438		708
	24.02	38.97		62.99
	591	533		1124
	52.58	47.42		

While the sex of the primary occupant is not associated with future intention, the duration of the stay is very related. Those who stay longer tend to be more satisfied, just as management anticipated. Once again, the summary test statistics confirm our informal analysis.

Test	ChiSquare	Prob>ChiSq
Likelihood Ratio	166.923	0.0000
Pearson	160.077	0.0000

Fisher's Exact	TestProb
Left	1.0000
Right	0.0000
2-Tail	0.0000

In order to get a better impression of the relationship between the duration of the stay and future intentions, we can do a little better than just categorize the predictor. (Logistic regression, often covered in a subsequent course, shows how to fit a model measuring how the response depends upon the duration. For now, we will settle for a plot.)

The plot that we want to view is a plot of the proportion who intend to return versus the length of stay. Basically, this plot is a continuous version of what we just did in the table. Using the *Fit Y by X* command with *Will Return?* as Y and *DaysStay* as (nominal) X gives the following plot (along with a huge table, which is not shown). Noting that the Yes category is on the top, we can see that the proportion who say "yes" grows steadily as the duration of stay increases.

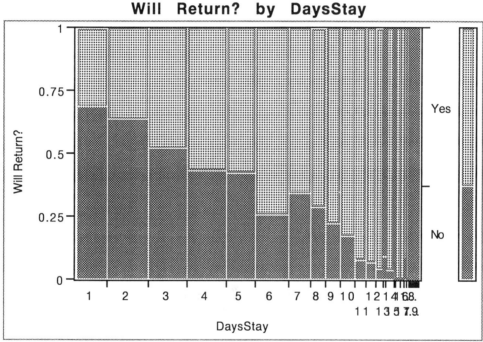

We can make a nicer version of this same plot by building a summary table. For this summary, we will use the variable *Satisfaction* which is coded as a "dummy variable":

Satisfaction = 1 if Will Return? = Yes,

Satisfaction = 0 if Will Return? = No.

This type of numerical encoding is quite important in regression analysis.

Now use the *Group/Summary* command from the *Tables* menu, and use *DaysStay* as the group factor and Mean(Satisfaction) as the Stats term. The resulting table looks like this:

Survey1.jmp by DaysStay

DaysStay	N Rows	Mean(Satisfaction)
1	103	0.310680
2	136	0.360294
3	128	0.476562
4	127	0.566929
...		
38	1	1
39	1	1
41	1	1
47	1	1

A plot of the Mean(Satisfaction), which is just the proportion who said yes, shows a strong trend:

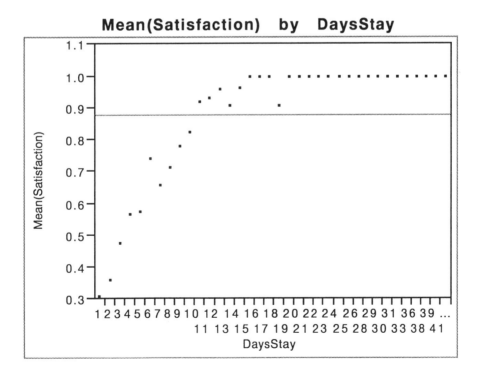

In order to verify the representativeness of the sample, the mean length-of-stay variable and the gender variable were compared to information that had been kept over the previous year (Survey2.jmp). This prior information relied upon accounting records only, so while it includes the sex of the primary customer and the length of stay, it *does not include* the customer's intention to return. The gender composition in the survey of guests was found to be in reasonable agreement with a sample of 1000 prior records (72.7% in this sample of 1000 were male versus 70.5% in the survey in June). However, the mean length of stay in the survey was approximately twice as long as that found from the sample of prior records (6.7 days versus 3.4 days).

Here are plots and summaries of data sampled from the list of guests during the prior year:

Sex

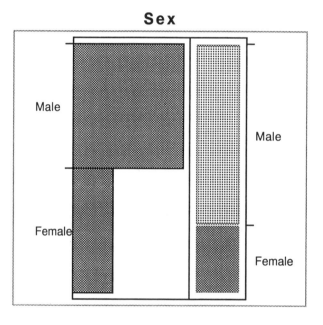

Frequencies

Level	Count	Probability	Cum Prob
Female	273	0.27300	0.27300
Male	727	0.72700	1.00000
Total	1000		

DaysStay

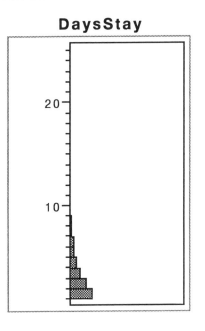

Quantiles

maximum	100.0%	25
quartile	75.0%	4
median	50.0%	2
quartile	25.0%	1
minimum	0.0%	1

Moments

Mean	3.397
Std Dev	3.065
Std Err Mean	0.097
upper 95% Mean	3.587
lower 95% Mean	3.207
N	1000

Given this confusion, the management of the hotel chain was uncertain as to the validity of its primary survey variable, the "intent to return." Had something gone horribly wrong? Could there be bias in the sampling procedure? But if so, then why did the sex variable agree with earlier figures?

The answer: the sampling scheme used to build the survey was flawed. Interviewing all those customers who were present on a particular day caused an overrepresentation of those who stayed for long lengths of time, known as "size-biased sampling." Size-biased sampling occurs in many domains and is not limited to hotel surveys or business. For example, consider estimating the population mean length of fish caught through drag nets. Small fish go right through the holes and are not represented in the sample.

The sex of the respondents is nonetheless representative because gender is not associated with length of stay. Women seem to stay just as long as men, as is displayed in the following table:

Crosstabs

Long Stay? Count Total %	Female	Male		
No	173	418	|	591
	15.39	37.19	|	52.58
Yes	158	375	|	533
	14.06	33.36	|	47.42
	331	793	|	1124
	29.45	70.55		

The proportion of women who opt to stay for a long visit is about 48%, whereas the corresponding proportion of men is about 47%.

The data for intent to return, however, are seriously in error because they are associated with the length-of-stay variable. Those who stay longer are more likely to return; conversely, those who have short stays are less likely to return. (Maybe they had a bad experience.)

In this problem, though, we are fortunate in that we can actually "patch up" the survey results to some extent. The problem with the survey is that customers who stayed for a long visit were oversampled; the longer someone stayed in the hotel, the more likely they are to be included in the survey. The solution here is to weight the observations, downweighting those who have stayed longer to compensate for the selection bias.

JMP makes it easy to do a weighted analysis. First, form a new column in the data file for the first survey (Survey1.jmp). Make this column a formula holding the reciprocal of *DaysStay*. Then, using the buttons at the top of this new column, mark it as a Weight variable. Now the summaries look different. Below is a comparison of the unweighted and weighted marginal statistics for length of stay.

	DaysStay Not Weighted	Weighted
Mean	6.701	3.473
Std Dev	5.614	1.798
Std Error Mean	0.167	
Upper 95% Mean	7.030	
Lower 95% Mean	6.372	
N	1124	1124
Sum Weights	1124	323.664

With the weights in place, the adjusted mean is now very close (3.47 versus 3.4) to the value obtained by sampling the guest records of the previous year. (Beware: the standard error is not comparable to that from the unweighted survey.)

Below is the summary of the crucial satisfaction variable, again weighted to adjust its value for oversampling those who stayed longer. Use the 0–1 variable *Satisfaction* to see the effect of weighting.

	Satisfaction Not Weighted	Weighted
Mean	0.630	0.470
Std Dev	0.483	0.268
Std Error Mean	0.014	
Upper 95% Mean	0.658	
Lower 95% Mean	0.602	
N	1124	1124
Sum Weights	1124	323.664

Thus, it seems that the hotel should not be so happy about the satisfaction level of its customers as the first, size-biased survey would imply. Weighting suggests that slightly less than half would be inclined to return, in comparison to the 63% suggested initially.

Currently the only information collected on the clientele is taken from voluntary customer satisfaction surveys that are left in hotel rooms; only 10% of guests complete the forms. Management is of the opinion that these surveys do not genuinely reflect customer feelings because only very angry or very happy customers fill them out.

How can the chain use a survey to learn more about its guests and their future travel plans?

For the hotel chain to get reliable information from a survey, it must avoid the problem of length biased sampling. In this case, since the length of stay is related to the intent-to-return response, the estimate of the proportion who plan to return is likely to considerably overstate the number of return visits. Also, the mean length of stay was off by a factor of two. This is a dramatic bias and has been observed in practice. Surveys often have hidden biases.

The example includes an application of weighting to repair the damages. Another approach would be to *stratify* the data. First, use the survey to learn the satisfied proportion of customers who stay for one day, two days, and so forth. Then use the previous accounting records to weight these satisfaction proportions by the proportion of clients who stay for a day, two days, and so on. This stratifying scheme will also correct for the fact that the survey has placed too much emphasis on customers who have stayed for a long visit.

Class 7. Making Decisions

In quality problems, we need to be assured that the process is functioning as designed. Therefore, ideas related to the confidence interval for the process mean are fundamental. In making a decision between two competing alternatives, we find that new issues arise.

Statistics provides a number of tools for reaching an informed choice (informed by sample information, of course!). Which tool, or statistical method, to use depends on various aspects of the problem at hand. When we make a choice between two alternatives, questions such as

Is there a standard approach?,

Is there a status quo?,

What are the costs of incorrect decisions?, and

Are such costs balanced?

become paramount.

Topics
> Hypothesis tests; null and alternative hypotheses
>
> Two-sample tests
>
> Checking assumptions
>
> False positives and false negatives (also called Type I and Type II errors)
>
> One-sided and two-sided comparisons
>
> Evidence versus importance; statistical significance versus substantive importance

Examples
> Effects of re-engineering a food processing line
>
> Selecting a painting process
>
> Analysis of time for service calls

Key Application

Should we switch treatments? The evaluation of various health-care procedures is one area in which statistics excels as a methodology for making careful and informed decisions. Take, for example, an HMO that is trying to decide between a presently accepted treatment for a disease and a newer but slightly more expensive one. Clearly, it makes no sense for the HMO to pay for the new treatment unless there is unambiguous evidence that it is better than the existing one.

Evidence is often collected in the health-care industry through the use of clinical trials. The analysis of the data from such trials provides the basis on which to make the decision. Ideally, these clinical trials have a built-in element of randomness — patients should be assigned to either the new or the old treatment at random — to ensure that there is no systematic bias in the samples. Obviously, the trial would be corrupted if all the really sick patients got the new treatment. Because of this intentionally introduced randomness, there is variability in the outcome measurements, that is two different samples of 100 patients would not respond exactly the same to the new treatment.

Now suppose that the sampled patients do in fact respond better to the new treatment than the old treatment. Because of the inherent variability in the data, the question will remain of whether or not the observed improvement represents a "genuine improvement" or if it could be explained by chance alone. That is, is the difference we observe just due to the inherent noise in the data or is there really a signal there?

Another way of thinking about this question is to consider what would happen if we ran the clinical trial again. How sure are we that the new treatment would beat the old treatment next time? To answer this question of whether or not the observed difference is real or if it may be accounted for by the inherent variability in the data, we use the idea of *statistical inference*. The first example we will encounter is called the two-sample t-test. It is rather ubiquitous. It answers the question of whether two population means are the same or different based on two samples, one from each population. In the context of the clinical trial, if we found no reason to reject the fact that the mean survival time for the new treatment was the same as the mean survival time for the present treatment, then there would be no reason to switch treatments.

Definitions

Hypothesis testing. This is the method that enables one to make a decision between two options in the presence of uncertainty.

Null hypothesis. The choice out of the two options that defines the status quo. Often it is the option whose choice would lead you to change nothing. It is the assumption that the null hypothesis is true that allows us to compute a *p*-value.

Alternative hypothesis. Typically, the option whose choice would lead you to change something — to alter the status quo, switch brands, switch to a new medical treatment, invest in a new company, and so on. In many cases, it may be the option that you hope to show is true.

p-value. The *p*-value is a measure of the credibility of the null hypothesis. Small *p*-values give you evidence against the null hypothesis. Large *p*-values suggest there is no evidence in the data to reject the null hypothesis; a large *p*-value implies that the data and null hypothesis are consistent with one another.

Concepts

Hypothesis testing and p-values. Hypothesis testing is an important part of statistics: it is a decision-making apparatus. In fact, statisticians often call decision-making *statistical inference.* The *p*-value is a simple statistical summary of a hypothesis test and can be used as the basis from which to make a decision. The *p*-value is the probability of seeing a sample like the one being viewed under a set of assumptions. When this probability is small, we infer that an assumption is wrong.

Using a confidence interval for inference. Many hypothesis tests turn out to be closely related to a confidence interval. Confidence intervals can produce identical decisions or inferences. We stress the confidence interval approach to hypothesis testing in this course because it focuses attention on the variability in the data and contains more information than the simple yes/no answer to a hypothesis test. Also, the confidence interval is a statement about where a population feature, such as the population mean, lies rather than a statement about what this parameter is not.

Heuristics

Counting standard errors. Many test statistics, for example the *t*-statistic, can be interpreted as standard error counters. For example, the two-sample *t*-test makes its decision based on how many standard errors the difference between the means is away from zero (zero difference implies the means are the same). The empirical rule tells us that if the true difference between the means is 0, then 95% of the time the observed difference between the sample means should be within ±2 standard errors from zero. That is why we call a *t*-statistic *extreme* if it is larger than 2 or less than –2.

The *p*-value is yet another way of describing how many standard errors the observed difference between the means is from zero. Extreme *t*-statistics are associated with small *p*-values, and nonextreme *t*-statistics(for example, *t*-statistics that lie between –2 and 2) are associated with larger *p*-values.

Confidence intervals and hypothesis tests. Hypothesis testing and confidence intervals have much in common. Remember that the purpose of the hypothesis test is to make a decision between two options. For the two-sample *t*-test again, the null hypothesis is usually that the means are the same or equivalently that the difference between the means is zero. Consequently, the null hypothesis can be operationalized through the question "Is zero a credible value for the difference between the means?" However, we know the range of feasible or credible values for the difference between the means; it is given by the confidence interval. So to see if zero is a credible value, we merely have to see if it lies in the confidence interval. If it does, then there is no reason to reject the null hypothesis; if it does not, then the data suggest that we reject the null hypothesis and go with the alternative one, concluding that the means are different (that their difference is not zero) and taking whatever action the alternative implies.

Potential Confusers

For many students, everything suddenly gets confusing at this point. Hang in there! A common point of confusion is the choice of which is to be the null hypothesis and which is to be the alternative hypothesis. The null hypothesis is more often the conjecture associated with leaving things alone, not making a change, or preserving the status quo. The alternative embodies doing something different, changing the way things have been done.

Selecting a Painting Process

Primer.jmp

Two processes are available for applying primer to the metal frames of cars coming down the assembly line. The goal is for the primer to be 1.2 mils (thousandths of an inch) thick.

Which process ought to be used?

The data available give the thickness in mils of primer applied to a sample of 110 cars. The sample sizes are not "balanced" – one sample has more data than the other. In this data, 50 observations are available for process *a* and 60 for process *b*.

Since these data were collected over time, we need to check for independence of the values within each process. We also need to verify that the processes are in control *before* doing continuing with the comparison. A chart of the process frequencies (the histogram of *Process*) makes it easy to subset the data and use the overlay plots to get sequence plots for each. These charts are shown on the next page.

We begin with a histogram of the process variable and select the bin showing the data for process *b*. This bin in highlighted in the figure below.

Process

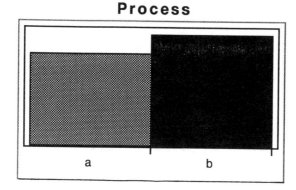

We next choose the *Exclude* and *Hide* commands from the *Rows* menu. (We need to do both of these to have the desired effect.) Now when we plot the data using *Fit Y by X* (Y = *Thickness*, X = *Sequence*), we see only those values that are associated with process *a*. Those cases from the process *b* are not used.

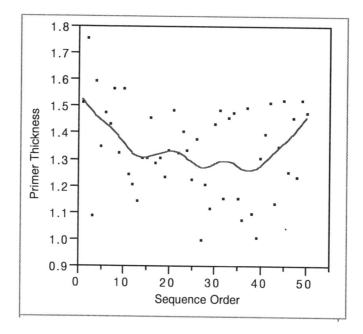

The data are quite irregular, but the smoothing spline (with lambda = 100) suggests some slight trend near the ends of the data sequence. These might deserve some follow-up.

Similar results hold for the 60 measurements from process *b*. We first clear the row states, then select the cell for process *a* and exclude and hide these.

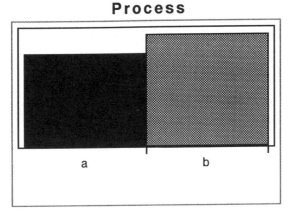

Once again, the *Fit Y by X* scatterplot shows the data to be irregular, with little evident trend other than the upward trend in the smoothing spline near the end of the series. This trend might be due to the two large positive outliers rather than a systematic change in the underlying process.

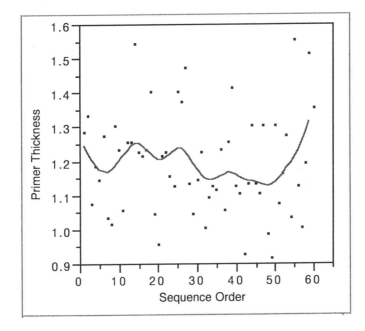

Let's hold off further discussion of the small trends in the data for both processes and assume for our purposes that these patterns are not serious.

The simplest way to compare these two batches uses the plot linking features of JMP. With a view of the histogram of all of the thickness data visible, simply click on the two categories of the process histogram to highlight the associated subsets in the histogram. This highlighting "animation" makes it clear that the average thickness from process *a* is quite a bit higher than that from process *b*. The two views of the thickness histogram with the associated subsets follows.

Histogram with process a selected

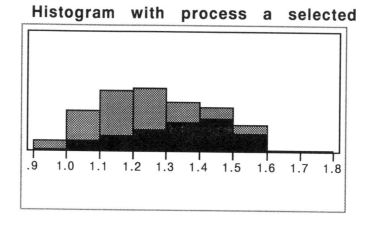

Histogram with process b selected

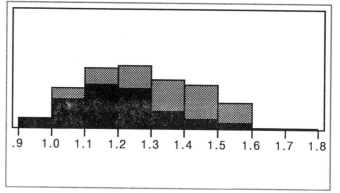

To get the details for each group, we can once again exclude subsets and construct separate histograms for each. Notice that the 95% confidence interval for the mean of process *a*, [1.296, 1.391] does not include the target value of 1.2 mils. The interval from process *b* is right on target.

Primer Thickness for Process A

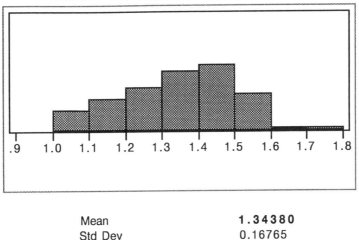

Mean	**1.34380**
Std Dev	0.16765
Std Err Mean	0.02371
upper 95% Mean	1.39144
lower 95% Mean	1.29616
N	50

Primer Thickness for Process B

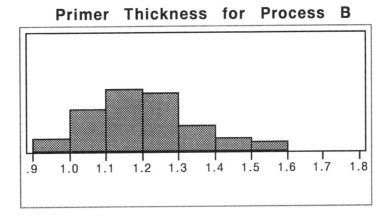

Mean	**1.19750**
Std Dev	0.15000
Std Err Mean	0.01937
upper 95% Mean	1.23625
lower 95% Mean	1.15875
N	60

The confidence intervals imply that the mean thickness for process *a* is too large (certainly in the initial periods) whereas the mean for process *b* is on target. Another way to address these same issues is to use a hypothesis test, as noted at the end of the motor shaft example in Class 5. For each process, we can compare its sample mean to the target thickness of 1.2 mils. The control for generating this test is at the top of the window showing the histogram of the thickness data for each process. If we choose the "Test mean = value..." item and enter 1.2 for the hypothesized value, we obtain the following summary for process *a* :

Hypothesized Value	1.2
Actual Estimate	1.3438
t Test	
Test Statistic	6.0652
Prob > ltl	<.0001
Prob > t	<.0001
Prob < t	1.0000

This test statistic 6.065 (known as a *t*-statistic and computed as (1.3438–1.2)/0.0237) indicates that the sample average, 1.34, is slightly more than 6 standard errors away from the hypothesized value, the target of 1.2 mils. This is too far to be a chance event; the output indicates that deviations of this size are virtually impossible. For process *b*, the corresponding *t*-test gives these results:

Hypothesized Value	1.2
Actual Estimate	1.1975
t Test	
Test Statistic	-0.1291
Prob > ltl	0.8977
Prob > t	0.5511
Prob < t	0.4489

For process *b*, the mean is only about $1/10$ of a standard error below the target. Deviations of a sample mean of this size (or larger) above or below the population mean are quite common and happen in about 90% of all samples. Certainly, this difference is no evidence that the mean of the process differs from 1.2.

In both cases, the results are consistent with our inferences drawn from confidence intervals. For process *a*, the sample mean is more than 2 standard errors away from 1.2 so that 1.2 does *not* lie in the confidence interval and is *not* a reasonable value for the population mean for process *a*. In contrast, 1.2 is only about 0.1 SE's away from the sample mean and very well could be the process mean. Certainly, the data offer little that would contradict this conjecture.

At this point we have found that process *b* is achieving the desired thickness and process *a* is not. Since both have roughly the same level of variation (if the SDs were very different, the choice would not be so clear), the choice seems clear: use process *b*. Without a default course of action, or a status quo to respect, we base our choice on the obvious: choose the process whose average is closer to the desired target (again, noting that the two are otherwise comparable in terms of variation).

However, suppose that process *a* is the one that is installed in our plants, and we will face considerable cost in making a changeover from one method to the other. In this situation, adopting process *b* will lead to retooling and retraining expenses. With this bias in favor of retaining process *a* , what can we conclude?

Since the goal is a primer thickness of 1.2 mils, we need to compare which process is coming closer. For this example, we will use the absolute deviation from the target thickness as our criterion. (These terms are stored as formulas in the data file.) The *Fit Y by X* platform offers a variety of ways to compare the two sets of absolute deviations. In particular, we can test whether the data show enough evidence to convince us that the two methods really do produce consistent differences in deviation from the target thickness. Perhaps the differences observed in the data are chance fluctuations.

The comparisons offered here, first graphically and then by hypothesis tests, make it clear that the difference between the two samples seen here is quite real. The fact that the intervals constructed in this example are disjoint indicates that the means of the two processes are significantly different.

It is important to realize that the confidence intervals shown as means diamonds in the following plot are *not* those that we would obtain were we to build intervals for the process deviation from the target for these two methods separately. As the JMP output on the next page indicates, these intervals rely upon an assumption: namely that the two samples are of comparable variance. In this example, the sample standard deviations, which estimate the process SDs, differ by about 50%. Unlike the process thicknesses, the absolute deviations have different SDs. We can build separate intervals "by hand" that avoid this assumption by using the standard errors reported in the JMP output.

Abs Deviation by Process

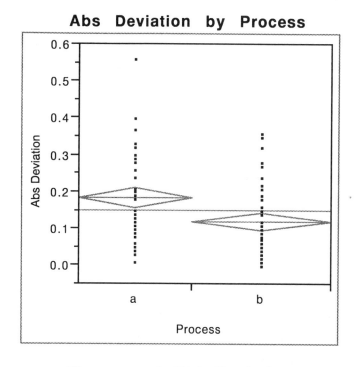

Means and Std Deviations

Process	Number	Mean	Std Dev	Std Err Mean
a	50	0.1834	0.122001	0.01725
b	60	0.1208	0.087514	0.01130

Rather than comparing the separate histograms and intervals, its better to consider the difference in the means directly, and one can use either an interval or test to make this comparison. The following output indicates that the 95% confidence interval for the difference in the two process means (for the absolute values) is [0.023, 0.102]. Since zero is outside this interval, the interval indicates that the mean for process *a* is larger than that for process *b*. Similarly, a *t*-test measures the distance between the two sample means and compares this distance to zero (by default). The *t*-statistic, as before, is simply a count of the number of standard errors that separates the two sample means from a hypothesized value, in this case zero. In this illustration, the difference between the two sample means is $t = 3.12$ SEs — quite a distance from zero based on the empirical rule.

t-Test

	Difference	t-Test	DF	Prob>ltl
Estimate	0.063	3.124	108	0.0023
Std Error	0.020			
Lower 95%	0.023			
Upper 95%	0.102			
Assuming equal variances				

The note in the JMP output at the bottom of the previous page makes it clear that the *t*-test requires the assumption of equal variances in the two groups being compared. However, we have already noted that the two sample standard deviations differ; the SD for process *a* is about 50% larger than that for process *b*.

We can check whether the two groups have different variances as well as different means, verifying or rejecting the assumption of the usual *t*-test. The difference between the variances is large, but the adjusted *t*-test (shown at the bottom and obtained by the *Unequal variances* item produced by the *Analysis* button) remains quite significant.

Tests that the Variances are Equal

Process	Count	Std Dev	MeanAbsDif to Mean	MeanAbsDif to Median
a	50	0.122	0.1024	0.1010
b	60	0.087	0.0703	0.0681

Test	F Ratio	DF Num	DF Den	Prob>F
O'Brien[.5]	4.8576	1	108	0.0296
Brown-Forsythe	6.5047	1	108	0.0122
Levene	8.4572	1	108	0.0044
Bartlett	5.8675	1	•	0.0154

Welch Anova testing Means Equal, allowing Std's Not Equal

F Ratio	DF Num	DF Den	Prob>F
9.2037	1	86.78	0.0032

t-Test

3.0338   **Adjusted t-statistic**

Two processes are available for applying primer to the metal frames of cars coming down the assembly line. The goal is for the primer to be 1.2 mils (thousandths of an inch) thick. Which process ought to be used?

Process *b* produces the desired primer thickness. Process *a* does not. The comparison of the two shown here using a hypothesis test indicates that the observed difference in mean deviation from target, as measured by sample averages, is evidence of a systematic difference between the two underlying processes rather than the consequence of merely sampling variation. In addition, the deviations of process *b* from the target are also less variable.

If process *a* is the current process, the decision of switching depends on how much the changeover will cost. The primer process currently in use applies a coating which is too thick — now we have to decide if it will be worth it to make the change.

We have not considered in this example the relevance of other issues that would also be important in choosing the better of two production processes. In addition to primer thickness, we might also be concerned about other factors such as

- cost of materials,
- complexity (and cost) of application equipment,
- time required to apply the primer, and
- durability of the paint.

Effects of Reengineering a Food Processing Line

FoodProc.jmp

A large food processing center needs to be able to switch from one type of package to another quickly to react to changes in order patterns. Consultants recommended and helped implement an alternative method for changing the production line.

Is this new changeover method faster than the old?

The data for both methods measure the time in minutes required to change the production on a food processing line. The data were gathered over time during prior days, and so each series is a time series of the time required to change production methods. Since the data are time series, we first check for trends.

Time series plots of the data from the two methods (shown on the next page) indicate some downward trend for both methods. In addition, the rapid up-and-down motion suggests that observations may be dependent. Finally, the variation of the data appears to change near the end of the time period of measurement.

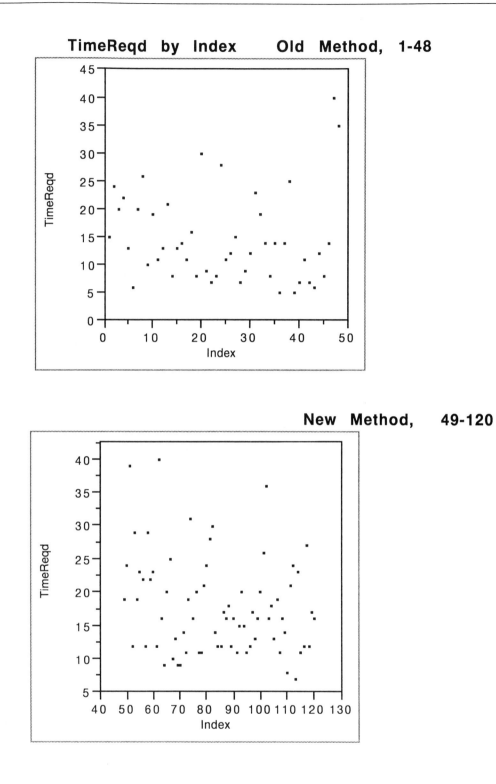

Assuming that we are not too concerned about the degree of trends or dependence seen in the time series plots, we can move on to comparing the averages. Plot linking gives a nice preliminary comparison of the two groups, suggesting that the old method (shown on the right below) takes longer. The highlighted portions of the histograms (shown in black) denote the data for the indicated subsets. The data also appear a bit skewed, as we might expect of timing data.

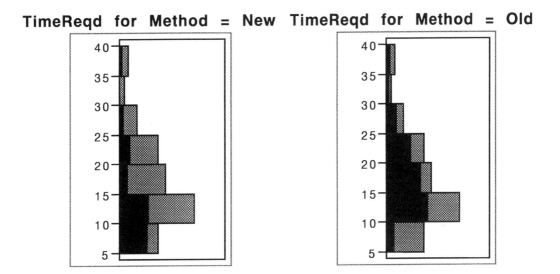

In some problems, such as this, there is a status quo that we would be inclined to retain unless the data convinced us that the new method is significantly better. In these cases, the status quo provides the basis for setting a null hypothesis — we are going to change to the new method only if it dominates the standard procedure.

Again assuming the absence of trends, we proceed to methods based on the *t*-statistic. The plot below from the *Fit Y by X* command shows two comparison boxplots. It seems clear that the old method is taking longer, as we noticed before. But is this observed sample difference indicative of a difference between the two processes from which these data are drawn, or really just a consequence of sampling variation?

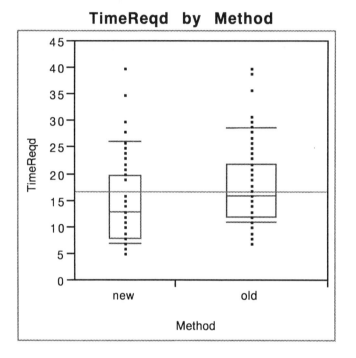

Ideally, at this point we would have access to some cost information. We would expect that each minute saved would be valuable, avoiding lost production time. However, how expensive would it be to install the new system and train all of the employees to use this method?

With the confidence intervals for the two means shown separately, we see just the very slightest overlap. Does this mean that the two methods are significantly different?

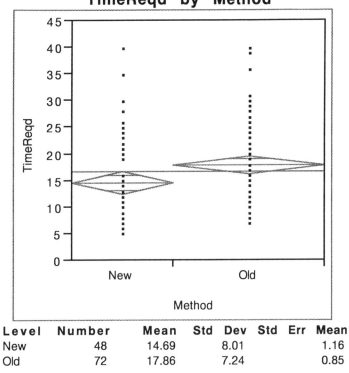

TimeReqd by Method

Level	Number	Mean	Std Dev	Std Err Mean
New	48	14.69	8.01	1.16
Old	72	17.86	7.24	0.85

As we mentioned in the previous example, the comparison implied by this plot is *not* the one that you want to use. The confidence intervals for the two means will not overlap if the upper end of the CI on the left is smaller than the lower end of the CI on the right, or

$$\bar{X}_{\text{new}} + \frac{2s_{\text{new}}}{\sqrt{n_{\text{new}}}} \; < \; \bar{X}_{\text{old}} - \frac{2s_{\text{old}}}{\sqrt{n_{\text{old}}}} \quad \Rightarrow \quad \bar{X}_{\text{new}} - \bar{X}_{\text{old}} < -\frac{2s_{\text{new}}}{\sqrt{n_{\text{new}}}} - \frac{2s_{\text{old}}}{\sqrt{n_{\text{old}}}} = -2(2.01) \, .$$

Since the difference in means is -3.17, the two are not different in this comparison. However, this is not the right procedure to use when comparing two means. It is simple to do, but it gets the wrong answer in some cases because it is a *conservative* procedure: if it finds a difference, you can be sure that one exists. However, it will miss some differences that you could detect if you used the right procedure. The right method is to use the standard error of the difference of the two means.

The *t*-test introduced in the previous example takes this approach. It compares the means based on the standard error of the difference in the means, rather than the overlap of two distinct confidence intervals. (It does, however, introduce an assumption: equal variation in the two groups.) The output below indicates that the observed methods have significantly different process means. The table shows the difference of the means (–3.17) and the associated standard error,

$$1.4 = SE(\overline{X}_{new} - \overline{X}_{old}) .$$

In particular, notice that the standard error of the difference in means is considerably smaller than the value associated with our previous comparison, 2.01. Consequently, this method finds a significant difference that the previous method missed.

The value in the *t*-test column is simply the ratio of these two, the observed difference divided by its standard error, –2.25 = –3.17/1.4. This size, namely larger than two, indicates a significant difference. Equivalently, notice that zero lies outside the interval — zero is not plausible.

t-Test

	Difference	t-Test	DF	Prob>ltl
Estimate	-3.174	-2.254	118	0.0260
Std Error	1.408			
Lower 95%	-5.962			
Upper 95%	-0.385			

Assuming equal variances

The standard deviations associated with the two methods are very similar, so we expect there to be little difference if we do not pool the data to estimate a common scale.

Means and Std Deviations

Level	Number	Mean	Std Dev	Std Err Mean
New	48	14.69	8.01	1.16
Old	72	17.86	7.24	0.85

JMP offers a variation on this comparison that does not require the assumption of equal variances in the two groups. (Select the *Unequal variances* item from the *Analysis* button.) If we do not pool, the t-statistic is -2.21 versus -2.25 based on pooling, and the two-sided *p*-values are comparable.

Welch Anova testing Means Equal, allowing Std's Not Equal

F Ratio	DF Num	DF Den	Prob>F
4.8778	1	93.714	0.0296
t-Test			
2.2086			

A large food processing center needs to be able to switch from one type of package to another quickly to react to changes in order patterns. Consultants recommended and helped implement an alternative method for changing the production line.

Is this new changeover method faster than the old?

The new changeover method is faster, and by a significant margin. The two-sided *p*-value is less than 0.03. A one-sided *p*-value would be half of this, giving a level of significance of less than 0.015.

An important property of confidence intervals is that they transform nicely. We found that the confidence interval for the difference in means is

$$[-5.96, -0.39].$$

If the cost per minute of lost production is $1000 and we make 20 changeovers per day, what is a confidence interval for the savings per day of using the new method? Finding it is easy: just multiply the previous interval by $1,000 \times 20$, giving

$$[\$7,800, \ \$119,200] .$$

We might save a lot, or very little, but we don't expect the new method to end up costing us more.

Analysis of Time for Service Calls

WaitTime.jmp

Two methods have been used to train service agents who make repairs to cellular telephone broadcast equipment. Which technique should be used in the future to get the job done most quickly?

During the last week, the company measured the time required to handle each of a sample of 150 calls for service. The calls were randomly divided into two groups, with 75 calls allotted to agents trained by the first method ("AAA") and 75 allotted to agents trained by the second ("Other"). For each sampled call, the time in hours to complete the service call was recorded.

As in the previous two examples, the most common methodology calls for an interval or test based on the mean and a *t*-statistic. The *t*-test makes three crucial assumptions of the data. The *t*-test assumes that the observations

        (1) are independent of each other,

        (2) arise from a normal population, and

        (3) have constant variance.

The connected time plot (not shown) shows no apparent trend or cyclical behavior. Evidently, assumption 1 is being met. Assumption 3 also appears reasonable in this example, although the data seem to have some periods of increased variation.

The assumption of normality is clearly violated, however. As you might expect, since are is waiting-time data, the distribution of the length of the service calls is rather skewed. The plot on the following page shows the distribution for all 150 observations together. It ought to be clear that "peeling off" outliers is not going to help in this problem; the underlying process (or processes) is not normal. The service time data are heavily skewed, with some calls lasting considerably longer than others. This degree of skewness affects the accuracy of the *t*-interval. The size of the distortion grows smaller, however, as the sample size increases. Although this sample is probably large enough for the t-interval to perform reasonably well, the severe skewness suggests that one consider a method based on the sample median.

Service   Time

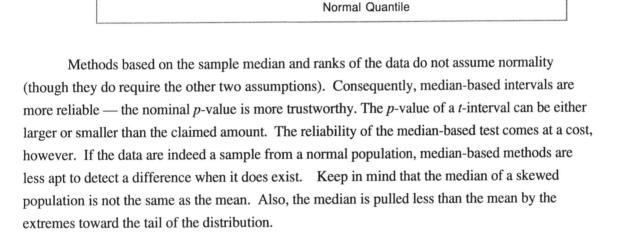

Methods based on the sample median and ranks of the data do not assume normality (though they do require the other two assumptions). Consequently, median-based intervals are more reliable — the nominal *p*-value is more trustworthy. The *p*-value of a *t*-interval can be either larger or smaller than the claimed amount. The reliability of the median-based test comes at a cost, however. If the data are indeed a sample from a normal population, median-based methods are less apt to detect a difference when it does exist.   Keep in mind that the median of a skewed population is not the same as the mean. Also, the median is pulled less than the mean by the extremes toward the tail of the distribution.

The displays on the next page give summaries for the two training methods. The two confidence intervals have considerable overlap. Note that the skewness persists in each group.

Service Time for AAA

Quantiles

quartile75.0%		2.800
median	50.0%	1.600
quartile25.0%		1.200

Moments

Mean	2.38
Std Dev	1.84
Std Err Mean	0.213
95% CI for Mean	1.95 — 2.80
N	75

Service Time for Other

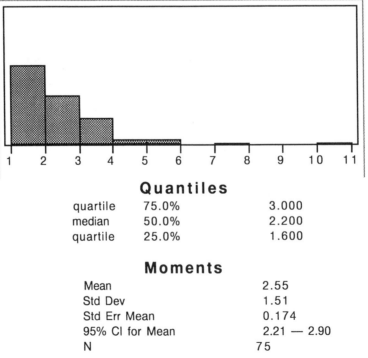

Quantiles

quartile	75.0%	3.000
median	50.0%	2.200
quartile	25.0%	1.600

Moments

Mean	2.55
Std Dev	1.51
Std Err Mean	0.174
95% CI for Mean	2.21 — 2.90
N	75

A comparison using mean-based methods confirms our initial impression. The two training methods lead to comparable service times. The now-familiar *t*-test indicates that the two means are not significantly different. The confidence intervals overlap to a large extent. In this example, the *p*-value is about 0.5, nowhere near the 0.05 reference.

Service Time by Training Program

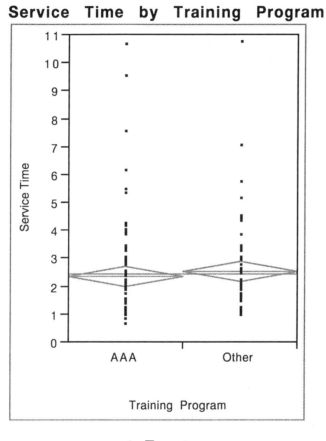

t-Test

t-Test	DF	Prob>|t|
0.65	148	0.52

Assuming equal variances

Program	N	Mean	Std Dev	Std Err Mean
AAA	75	2.376	1.843	0.213
Other	75	2.555	1.505	0.174

We know, however, that a sample mean is sensitive to outlying values. In the presence of many outliers and skewed data, the mean is not a reliable summary measure. In the summaries of the two groups, the median service time of the "Other" group is 0.6 larger than the median for the "AAA" group (the means differ by only 0.18). JMP offers a comparison test based on medians rather than means. The median test fails to find a significant difference, though the p-yalue is much smaller.

Median Test (Number of Points above Median)

Level	Count	Score Sum	Score Mean	(Mean-Mean0)/Std0
AAA	75	33	0.440	-1.302
Other	75	41	0.546	1.302

2-Sample Test, Normal Approximation

S	Z	Prob>|Z|
41	1.30215	0.1929

1-way Test, Chi-Square Approximation

ChiSquare	DF	Prob>ChiSq
1.6956	1	0.1929

One can make two types of errors in using hypothesis tests. The first error, the Type I error, occurs if we incorrectly reject the null hypothesis and conclude that the groups differ when in fact they are the same. The second error, the Type II error, is usually less emphasized and occurs when we fail to reject the null when it is false. Often one suffers a Type II error because the testing procedure is *inefficient* in its use of the data. Even though it makes sense, the median test just shown is not very efficient. Fortunately, JMP offers a test that is as efficient as the t-test but is not so distorted to skewness. This alternative comparison is based on ranking the data in the two groups. It does find the difference suggested by the medians to be significant, with a two-sided p-value of 0.020.

Van der Waerden Test (Normal Quantiles)

Level	Count	Score Sum	Score Mean	(Mean-Mean0)/Std0
AAA	75	-13.895	-0.185	-2.333
Other	75	13.895	0.1853	2.333

2-Sample Test, Normal Approximation

S	Z	Prob>|Z|
13.895	2.333	0.0197

1-way Test, Chi-Square Approximation

ChiSquare	DF	Prob>ChiSq
5.4413	1	0.0197

Two methods have been used to train service agents who make repairs to cellular telephone broadcast equipment. Which technique should be used in the future to get the job done most quickly?

A means-based comparison indicates that the two training methods are essentially equivalent, whereas the comparison based on ranks says that the "AAA" trainees complete the service calls significantly faster.

How are we to resolve this difference of opinion?

The issue comes down to how we are going to compare the two batches of numbers, and ultimately the two training methods. If we care only about which method tends to give the shorter time, then "AAA" is better since a random service call handled by these technicians will be shorter than a randomly chosen call handled by an "Other" trainee. However, it would be unwise to make an inference about the difference in the length of time required – there is simply too much variation. The "AAA" calls appear shorter, but the aggregate length of time in this comparison is indistinguishable because so much variation is present.

You have probably noticed that we used several tests in this analysis. Picking a test based on which one gives you the answer that you want is not a good idea — why bother with statistics if you already know the answer? We wanted to illustrate here how the tests compare rather than to suggest a strategy for "how to lie with statistics."

Class 8.   Designing Tests for Better Comparisons

The two-sample tests of Class 7 are not always the best choice. Often, specially designed experiments can be more informative at a lower cost (i.e., smaller sample size). As one might expect, using these more sophisticated procedures introduces trade-offs, but the costs are typically small relative to the gain in information.

When we are faced with a comparison of two alternatives, a test based on paired data is often much better than a test based on two distinct (independent) samples. Why? If we have done our experiment properly, the pairing lets us eliminate background variation that otherwise hides meaningful differences.

Topics

    Effects of paired measurements and association

    Scatterplots and dependence

    Matching and confounding

    Power of a test

    Design of experiments

Examples

    Taste test comparison of teas

    Pharmaceutical sales force comparison

Key Application

The effect of a pollution event on real estate prices. Suppose you are trying to figure out what impact a pollution event has had on a housing market. You know that in an area very similar to that in which the pollution event occurred house prices increased by 10% over a 5-year period that spanned the date at which the pollution occurred. The critical question is whether or not house prices in the pollution area have gone up by less than 10%. This information would help in assessing damages to award in a lawsuit. What is a good way of collecting the data on house price increases in the polluted area?

    One method would be to randomly sample 100 houses that were sold prior to the pollution event, and then to sample 100 that were sold after the pollution event and find the respective mean prices. Although this is not unreasonable, there is a potentially better way to collect the information. The idea is simple: to sample houses that had two sales, one sale prior to the pollution event and one after the pollution event.

The great advantage of this is that by collecting two observations on the same sampling unit (a house) it is possible to reduce the variability present in the data. The reason for this is that two observations on the same house are highly related even though prices between houses are highly variable. Just consider what would happen if you had a few mansions in the pre-event sales data and some duplexes in the post-event data. Taking repeat observations on the same unit and then differencing removes much of this unwanted variability in the data. The only thing we are interested in is "what is the rate of increase in house prices;" we do not want our search for this information corrupted by the fact that houses themselves are very variable in price.

So the theme of this class is that through a thoughtful sampling scheme it is possible to remove unwanted variability, or noise, from data. If we remove much of the noise, it is possible to see a signal more clearly if it does indeed exist.

The bottom-line benefit of using this "paired" sampling technique is that you can sometimes get more information for less money. How much better you do (i.e., how much money you save) by using a paired sampling scheme as opposed to taking two independent samples depends on how related the repeat observations are. The more dependence between the two repeat observations, the better you will do. If, in fact, the repeat observations are not at all dependent then you will gain no benefit from the paired sampling scheme and you might as well take two independent samples.

The idea of exploiting dependence has great value. Here we have seen it as a way of efficiently collecting data, and it works because house prices are positively related. That is, if the pre-pollution sale price is high then the post-pollution price is likely to be high; likewise, if the pre-pollution sale price is low then the post-pollution price is likely to be low. Exploiting dependence also lies at the heart of constructing low-risk portfolios, but this time we exploit negative dependence. The idea is that if you can find two stocks that are highly negatively related (that is, as one goes up the other goes down), then by buying both you decrease the variability of your return. You can apply the same idea to horse racing. Say you are going to place a bet well before the weather conditions are known. Betting on one horse that performs well on firm ground and one that performs well on soft ground makes your bet insensitive to the weather conditions on race day. What is happening here is that you are exploiting the negative dependence: if one of your horses does badly, then it increases the chances that the other one will do well.

Definition

Power. The power of a test is the probability of rejecting the null hypothesis under some set of stated conditions, such as a given difference of population means.

Concepts

Designing experiments. By carefully considering the structure, and in particular the dependence relationships that exist in data, it is possible to exploit this dependence in designing sampling schemes and get more information than if this dependence was ignored.

Power of a test. The power of a statistical hypothesis test is a number that lies between 0 and 1 (it is a probability). It tells how likely you are to reject the null hypothesis. In the context of the paired *t*-test, the power tells how likely you are to conclude there is a difference between the two groups when there really is a difference. The power depends on the difference. When the means are far apart, the power is larger than when they are close together (keeping other factors fixed).

Clearly, since power is a measure of doing the "right thing," we want the power of a test to be high. Imagine you had a test that had a power of 0.5 when the mean difference was 10. Then you would only have a 50–50 chance of detecting such a difference when it really did exist. You always have to remember that simply because we conclude that there is no difference between two groups does not show conclusively that there really is no difference. Maybe there is a difference, it is just small and the power of our test is low.

Heuristics

Low power. Discovering that a test has low power implies that it is not focused enough to see the signal through the noise. That is, you are not likely to find an important difference even if one exists.

Taste-Test Comparison of Teas

Taste.jmp

> Two formulations of a prepackaged iced tea have been proposed for a new beverage. Based on a taste test, which one should be taken to market, or do the results offer a compelling choice?

A small taste test was organized using 16 panelists from a focus group. Each panelist tasted both formulations and rated them on a scale of 1 (excellent) to 7 (would not drink if last thing in the fridge on a hot August day).

Since each panelist tastes both formulations, we ought to ask some related questions of how the data were collected. For example, did everyone taste formulation #1 first and then taste formulation #2? Doing so introduces an order effect that would lead to a *confounded* experiment. How would we know whether the results we obtain come from the tea or come from the order of presentation?

We begin with summaries of the two sets of evaluations. From the plots and summaries on the next page, it appears that the first formulation is preferred (i.e., has the lower scores), but is the difference large? There is clearly quite a bit of overlap in the two confidence intervals. Notice that the bins have been relocated to be centered on the integer ratings (use the *Hand* tool). Otherwise, which limit of the bin is being counted?

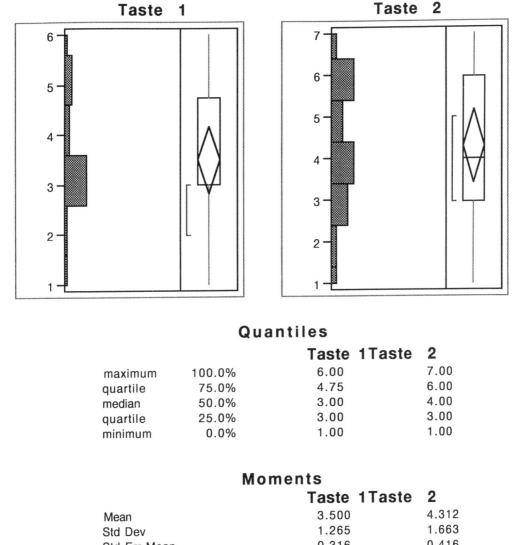

Quantiles

		Taste 1	Taste 2
maximum	100.0%	6.00	7.00
quartile	75.0%	4.75	6.00
median	50.0%	3.00	4.00
quartile	25.0%	3.00	3.00
minimum	0.0%	1.00	1.00

Moments

	Taste 1	Taste 2
Mean	3.500	4.312
Std Dev	1.265	1.663
Std Err Mean	0.316	0.416
upper 95% Mean	4.174	5.198
lower 95% Mean	2.826	3.427
N	16	16

How should we judge the size of the difference in the average ratings? Since the same panelists tasted both types of tea, it would not make sense to use the two-sample procedure from Class 7 since these data violate a critical assumption of the two-sample *t*-test, namely that the observations in the two groups are independent. Since each person rates both formulations, we expect some dependence in their evaluations.

It is more reasonable to expect that some panelists simply like tea better than others and will rate both higher. A scatterplot of the two sets of ratings (use the *Fit Y by X* command of the *Analyze* menu) shows that this is indeed the case.

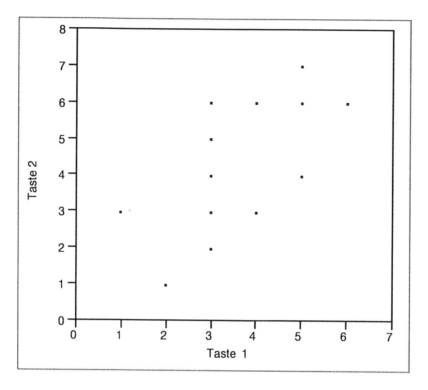

Where would the points fall if the two sets of measurements were identical? They would be on the 45° diagonal line. The test procedure we will use in this case measures how far the points fall from this line. If the two teas were the same, we would expect the panelists to give the same rating to each, with perhaps a bit of random variation. The points in the plot would then cluster along the diagonal line taste 1 = taste 2. This observation is the basis for the plot shown on the next page.

The paired *t*-test option at the bottom of the fitting menu adds several reference lines to the plot. The heavy line in the following figure is the reference line x = y. The points should cluster along this line if the two formulations are the same. How close should they be? The line between the two dashed lines is parallel to the reference line but constructed to pass through the point (mean of taste 1, mean of taste 2). The dashed lines represent a confidence interval. If the reference line lies outside the dashed lines, the two means are significantly different (two-sided, 95%). The numerical summary that accompanies the plots adds the usual details.

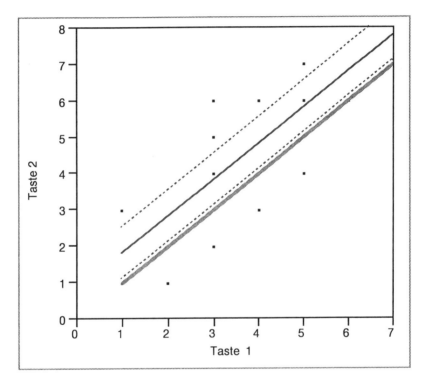

The numerical summary again uses the standard formulation of a t-test: count the number of standard errors that separate the observed difference from zero.

Paired t-Test

Taste 1 – Taste 2

Mean Difference	-0.8125	Prob > ltl	0.0271
Std Error	0.3318	Prob > t	0.9864
t-Ratio	-2.4480	Prob < t	0.0136
DF	15		

Two formulations of a prepackaged iced tea have been proposed for a new beverage. Based on a taste test, which one should be taken to market, or do the results offer a compelling choice?

The panelists significantly preferred the first formulation, a result we would have missed if we were to improperly analyze these data using a two-sample method.

Going further, it might make sense to add some additional information to the results of such a taste test. For example, one might suspect that preferences change as the subjects age. That is, a younger audience might prefer a sweeter formulation than an older collection of subjects (or perhaps not). Such an analysis provides the fundamental information needed when segmenting a market for purposes of advertising and other sorts of promotion.

Pharmaceutical Sales Force Comparison

PharmSal.jmp

Management of a newly merged pharmaceutical company needs to reduce its sales force. The sales force has two groups, one from each of the companies that were merged. Management would like to know if the sales force for the "GL" division differs from the sales force for the "BW" division.

Does one sales force outperform the other?

Data were available for the performance of the sales forces of the two firms, each with representatives in the "same" 20 sales districts selling what are essentially comparable drugs. (The districts are not identical but are rather comparable.)   The data appear normally distributed.

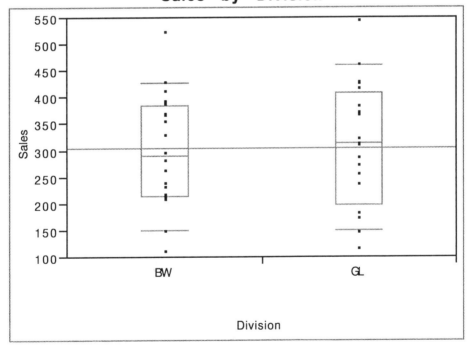

Sales   by   Division

Quantiles

Division	Min	10%	25%	median	75%	90%	Max
BW	112	151.1	215.25	291	385.5	428.5	525
GL	119	151.6	197.75	313.5	409.75	460.6	547

As suggested by the initial boxplots, the sales levels obtained in the 20 districts by each sales force are quite comparable. If we treat the data as two independent samples, we obtain quite similar values. The average sales are almost the same, with no evident significant difference ($t = 0.38$ implies that the two means only differ by less than $1/2$ of one SE).

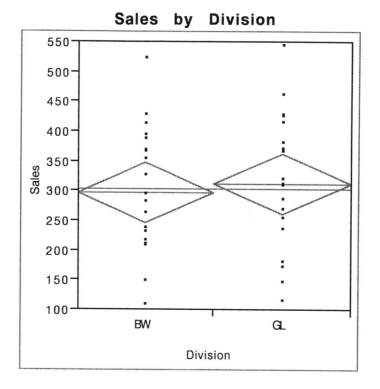

t-Test

	Difference	t-Test	DF	Prob>|t|
Estimate	-13.500	-0.380	38	0.7057
Std Error	35.484			
Lower 95%	-85.334			
Upper 95%	58.334			

Assuming equal variances

Div	Number	Mean	Std Error
BW	20	298.150	25.091
GL	20	311.650	25.091

This two-sample comparison ignores, however, the pairing introduced by the sales district factor. Both sales forces operate in the same districts. Each regional district has its own unique properties: some are more urban than others, some have more managed care facilities, etc. As a result, the sales levels obtained by the two groups are unlikely to be independent — districts with high sales for one division are likely to have high sales in the other division as well (or perhaps low sales if the two compete head-on).

We have two ways to rearrange our data as needed for this paired analysis. The initial data file has a single column, with the *Division* column indicating the sales force. We cannot do a paired analysis with the data as such; we need to rearrange the data to recognize the pairing. The elegant approach is to use the *Split columns* command of the *Tables* menu, splitting the sales column using *Division* as the *Column ID* variable (the values of *Division* — GL and BW — become the names of the columns in the new data table). This gives a new data table with the *Sales* variable split into two columns, each with 20 rows. In the new table, the data are paired by district. For this example, we could also just copy the last 20 rows of the *Sales* variable into a new column and make the comparison that way, but this approach fails if the rows are not nicely ordered.

With the data rearranged, a plot of the sales shows that there is a strong relationship between the corresponding levels of sales. Recall that you obtain a scatterplot such as this via the *Fit Y by X* command of the *Analyze* menu.

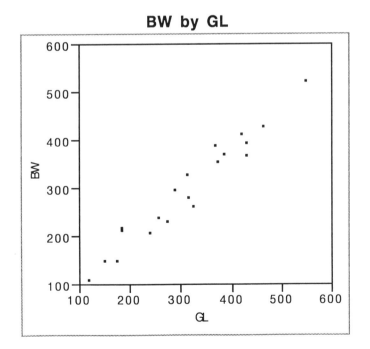

The paired *t*-test takes advantage of this natural pairing to obtain a more efficient — and correct — comparison of the two groups. The comparison uses the differences within each pair. The use of differences within districts removes much of the variation from the data and leads to our detecting significant difference in the sales levels obtained by the two sales forces. The high concentration of the sales along the diagonal indicates the large degree of association between the sales of the two groups: where one does well, so does the other.

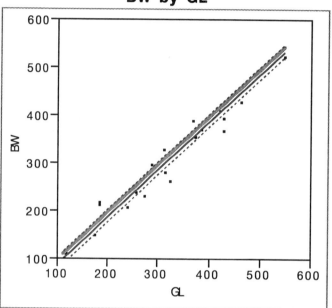

Though it's hard to tell from this figure (use the magnifying lens tool to expand the scale), the reference line *does* lie outside the 95% interval, so that the difference is significant. The tabular summary is more precise, and we can easily see that the two-sided *p*-value is less than 0.05.

Paired   t-Test
GL - BW

Mean Difference	13.50	Prob > ltl	**0.0360**	⇐
Std Error	5.98	Prob > t 0.0180		
t-Ratio	2.26	Prob < t 0.9820		
DF	19			

Management of a newly merged pharmaceutical business needs to reduce its sales force. It would like to know if the sales force for the "GL" division differs from the sales force for the "BW" division. Does one sales force outperform the other?

A comparison based on differences within districts detects a significant difference between the two sales forces. The GL division has a significantly higher level of sales. Without the pairing, the variation attributable to differences between regions conceals the consistent superiority of the GL group.

Remark

When data are paired as these districts are, it is often more simple to work with differences rather than pairs. The difference within each district indicates which of the two forces is doing better under comparable conditions. The confidence interval shown [0.98, 26.02] does not include zero — zero is an implausible value for the population difference in sales. Using the differences, however, conceals why this pairing is effective: sales across the districts are dependent.

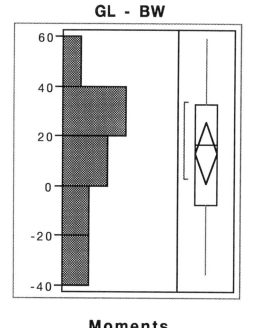

GL - BW

Moments

Mean	13.50
Std Dev	26.75
Std Err Mean	5.98
95% CI for Mean	[0.98, 26.02]
N	20

Since zero lies outside the 95% interval, the difference is significant. The reported *p*-value is the same (0.036) as that from the prior analysis.

Test Mean=value

Hypothesized Value	0	
Actual Estimate	13.5	
	t Test	
Test Statistic	2.257	
Prob > |t|	**0.036**	<--- same
Prob > t	0.018	
Prob < t	0.982	

Class 9.   Confounding Effects in Tests: A Case Study

Getting proper samples is often simply not possible. Particularly when making two-sample comparisons, one frequently discovers that the two samples differ in more ways than one expects. In this case study, we consider how such confounding factors influence the outcome of statistical tests and show how, with a little luck and the right questions, we can avoid the worst mistakes.

Topics
  Association, confounding, and matching

Example
  Wage discrimination

Key Application

Wage Discrimination. Suppose we wish to determine if there is systematic discrimination in wages between men and women. Ideally, if we see a difference between men and women, we want to attribute this difference to the fact that there is discrimination. However, just because we see a difference in wages, it does not necessarily follow that there is discrimination. It is possible that the observed difference in wages is due to other factors: for example men and women may have different levels of education and you might choose to attribute the difference in wages to the difference in education rather than to pure discrimination.

In order to make a strong statement about discrimination, we need to make sure that we have taken into account, as completely as possible, all the other variables and factors that may have an influence on wages. The best situation would be if we had virtually identical groups of men and women who were extremely similar in terms of all these other variables and differed only with respect to gender. If this were the case and we observed a wage difference between men and women, then we could unambiguously attribute it to gender since all other possible explanatory variables are identical for both sexes. Variables that you might want to take into account, or "control for" as a statistician would probably include years of experience, educational level, marital status, performance evaluation, and age. No doubt you can think of additional variables that influence someone's wages and which we call "explanatory variables." The process of trying to identify the variables that influence the object you are trying to measure, in this example wages, is very important because only after you have captured all these other variables can you identify the unique contribution to wages that is made by the particular explanatory variable in which you are interested, again in this example gender.

When the explanatory variables are related amongst themselves, we say that they are confounded. Under these circumstances, it can be extremely difficult to identify the important explanatory variables. One simple but effective way to achieve this is to "stratify the data." Stratification is the process by which a sample is split into smaller groups so that observations are similar *within* groups but different *between* groups. Splitting the sample into subgroups according to "years of experience" is an example of a stratification that might be useful in a wage discrimination case. Other possible variables by which you might want to stratify are "managerial level" and "highest attained qualification." The idea is that we should be comparing "like with like" and stratification helps achieve this effect.

Often good studies do this stratification or matching before the data are collected. For example, if we wanted to determine effectiveness of two different advertising campaigns used to get individuals to switch their long-distance carrier, it would be a good idea to match people according to telephone usage because how much you use the telephone will influence your interest in switching carriers.

One problem with stratification is that by the time you have stratified the data by a few variables, you tend to end up with very small numbers of observations and hence little information in each subgroup. Fortunately, there is a statistical technique that provides a cohesive way of dealing with confounding variables. It is called *regression*. Regression has many uses, but its ability to "control" for confounding variables is one of its most useful attributes. Nonetheless, regression is no substitute for a carefully designed and randomized experiment.

Definitions

Response variable. The variable we are trying to understand, predict, or identify its sources of variability. JMP calls it the Y variable because it would be plotted on the Y-axis (the vertical one) of a scatterplot.

Explanatory variable. We call a variable explanatory if we think it may help to explain the variability in the response variable. JMP calls this an X variable (on the horizontal axis) because it would be plotted on the X-axis of a scatterplot.

Marginal association. We call the association between a single explanatory variable (gender) and a response variable (wages), ignoring all other possible explanatory variables, the marginal association.

Partial association. We call the relationship between a single explanatory variable (gender) and a response variable (wages) after having taken into account other possible explanatory variables (e.g., education, experience) the partial association.

Confounding. Our inability to attribute an observed effect, such as a difference in wages, to some explanatory factor, such as sex, because of the presence of other uncontrolled factors (such as age or experience).

Concepts

Confounded variables. These are measurements that are related to each other. Typically, only one of these is actually observed. For example, suppose we want to compare two teachers by seeing how well their students compare on a common final exam. If we just compare scores at the end of the term, we have omitted an important factor, namely how good the students were at the start of the term. This factor confounds our results since it also explains the difference in final test scores.

Association is not the same as causation. It is very easy to fall into the trap of believing that when we find a difference between two groups, that difference is caused or attributable to the two labels we have put on the groups. So in the above example, just because we see a difference in wages between men and women (wages and gender are associated), it does not follow that gender is causing this difference. There may always be a third variable, confounded and perhaps even unmeasured, that is the real reason for the difference between the groups, and it just happens to be associated with gender. Two variables may be related because of the effects of a third variable, what is known as *spurious association.* The observed difference between average wages for men and women in the following example need not imply that sex is causing the difference in wages. Perhaps, as we shall see, the difference is due to some other factor, such as skill or age or level of experience.

While it's easy to invent such explanations for observed relationships, one is not entirely free in this choice. An important property of indirect relationships is that if the intervening factor is causing the spurious association that we see, then the associations between the hidden factor and the observed variables must be higher than the observed association between the two variables in question. For example, if there is some factor, say genetics, that is producing the association between smoking and lung cancer, then the association between smoking and genetics *and* the association between lung cancer and genetics both need to be stronger than the association we observe between smoking and lung cancer.

Potential Confuser

Simpson's paradox. Marginal association is not the same as partial association. Baseball fans might find this explanation intuitive. Consider two batters, *A* and *B*. Suppose that *A* has a higher batting average than *B* against *both* right and left handed pitchers. This dominance does not, however, imply that batter A has the higher overall average. It is possible that B has the higher batting average. How can this happen? One possible explanation is that batter *A* has faced more of one type of pitcher, say left-handed pitchers, than batter *B*, and that it is harder to get a hit off these pitchers. Though worse against either left-handed or right-handed pitchers, *B* has the higher overall average since *B* has faced more easy-to-hit pitchers. In this example, the batting averages against left/right-handed pitchers reflects a type of partial association, whereas the overall averages reflect the marginal association.

Wage Discrimination

Salary.jmp

A business magazine has done a large survey that appears to indicate that mid-level female managers are being paid less than their male counterparts.

Is this claim valid?

To resolve this claim, data were gathered on a sample of 220 randomly selected managers from firms. The data file has the following format. It includes row markers that define colors and markers that appear in plots (red boxes for the women and blue +'s for the men).

Salary	Sex	Position	YearsExper	Sex Codes	Mid-Pos?
148	male	7	16.7	1	0
165	male	7	6.7	1	0
145	male	5	14.8	1	1
139	female	7	13.9	0	0
...					
147	male	5	8.8	1	1
156	male	7	15.1	1	0
132	male	4	4.7	1	1
161	male	7	16.5	1	0

The variables represented by these columns are defined as follows:

Salary   Base annual compensation, in thousands of $U.S.

Sex   Pretty obvious.

Position   An index for the rank of the employee in the firm; roughly corresponds to the number of employees supervised by the individual, size of budget controlled, etc., so that higher positions imply higher rank.

Years Exp Number of years of relevant experience for current position.

Sex Code   A dummy variable, with 0 for females and 1 for males (formula column).

Mid-Pos?   A dummy variable, with 1 for positions 4 to 6, zero otherwise (formula).

We begin by considering the marginal distribution of salary for this sample of mid-level managers. The salaries range from $110,000 to $172,000, with an average of $142,860. The initial histogram appears to be somewhat bimodal, with the histogram showing perhaps two areas of peak concentration.

Salary

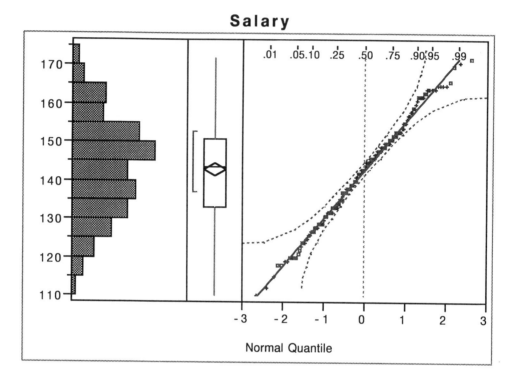

Normal Quantile

Quantiles

maximum	100.0%	**172.00**
quartile	75.0%	151.00
median	50.0%	143.50
quartile	25.0%	133.00
minimum	0.0%	**110.00**

Moments

Mean	**142.86**
Std Dev	12.52
Std Error Mean	0.84
Upper 95% Mean	144.53
Lower 95% Mean	141.20
N	220

By shifting the locations of the histogram bins (use the *Hand* tool accessed from the *Tools* menu), it appears that the bimodality is not a very meaningful feature of the data. The bimodal shape occasionally disappears as we shift the origin of the bins.

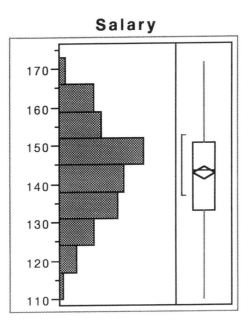

The bimodal appearance of the initial histogram is also rather muted when we superimpose the smooth density.

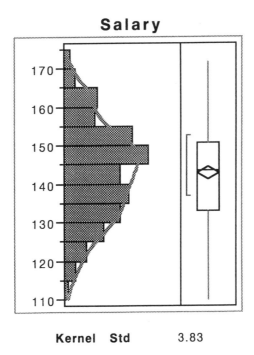

For these data, 145 of the 220 managers are men. Keeping the histogram of this column on the screen makes it easy in the subsequent analysis to highlight the observations from each sex, as in the two views of the marginal distribution.

Sex

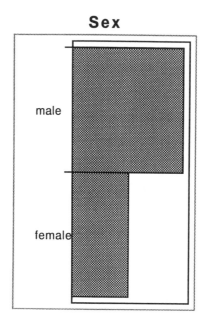

Salary

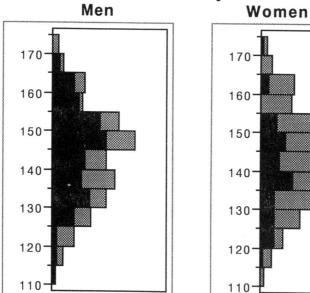

The two-sample *t*-test comparison indicates that, on average, men are paid more than $3,600 more than the women in this sample. The two-sample comparison via the *t*-test or confidence interval indicates that this difference is significant. The confidence interval does not include zero; the *p*-value is 0.04 (two-sided). The mean salaries in the two respective populations are not likely to be the same.

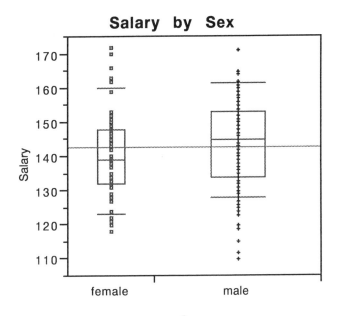

t-Test

Difference	t-Test		DFProb>ItI	
Estimate	-3.64	-2.061	218	0.0405
Std Error	1.77			
Lower 95%	-7.13			
Upper 95%	-0.16			

Assuming equal variances

Means

Level	Number	Mean	Std Error
female	75	140.467	1.4351
male	145	144.110	1.0321

Std Error uses a pooled estimate of error variance.

A more thorough analysis recognizes that there are other differences between the men and women aside from gender alone. For example, the men have more years of experience than the women and tend to occupy higher positions. Since the intervals of the two groups do not overlap, the differences are significant (given that one believes the underlying assumptions, of course).

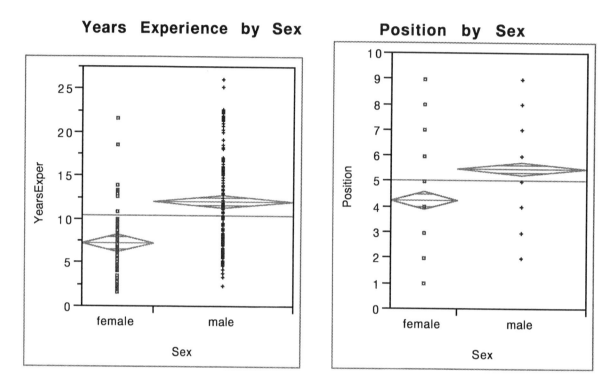

Both of these factors, years of experience and position, offer some explanation for the difference in salary between men and women. Each is related to gender, and the relationships are stronger than that we have observed between sex and salary. A concept covered later, known as correlation (Class 10), will help quantify the strength of the association, but from looking at the graphs the means in the two groups are clearly very distinct, more so than the means of salary for men and women. Now we need to check the second linkage required for an indirect factor, namely that for either of these to be the "hidden factor," each must be associated with salary. These plots are on the next page.

Note: Beware of plots of discrete data such as that of *Position* on *Sex*. Each point in the figure typically represents quite a few observations because of the discrete nature of the position data.

Other differences between the two groups would be irrelevant were it not for the fact that these other factors might be related to salary (as well as to each other). The horizontal lines in the figure are the averages of the two groups.

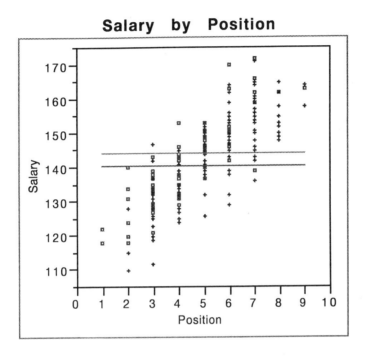

Men tend to predominate the right of the plot, with women more concentrated on the left.

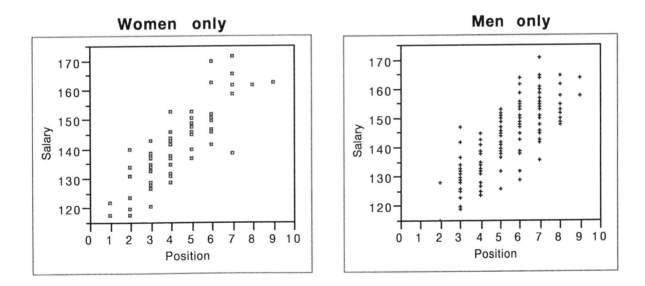

We have seen that *Salary* is clearly related to *Position*. *Salary* is also related to years of experience, but the association is not so clear graphically. We'll continue with *Position* as our prime candidate for explaining the observed differences between the salaries of men and women.

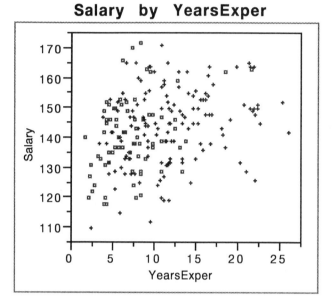

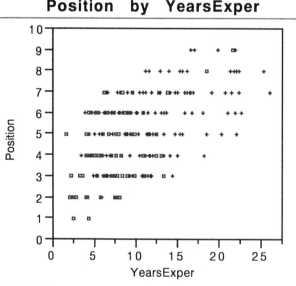

It appears, then, that the two samples are perhaps not comparable. For example, the men occupy positions that pay more and they have more experience. One means of trying to remove the effect of such differences is to consider smaller, more homogeneous subsets of the data. The *Mid-Pos?* factor identifies the 116 employees whose position lies in the range from 4 to 6.

With several linked histograms side by side, we can see which managers these are.

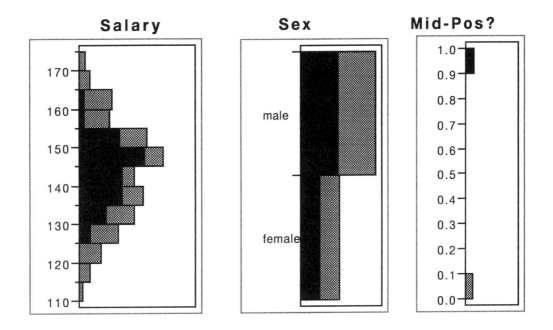

With the analysis restricted to this subset, we get a different impression of the differences in compensation. The results on the next page suggest that men are paid less than women in comparable positions! The ordering of the sample means has been reversed, with the men in this subset making on average more than $2,000 less than the women. This time, however, the difference is not significant. The *p*-value (two-sided) is 0.20 and the 95% confidence interval includes zero.

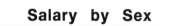

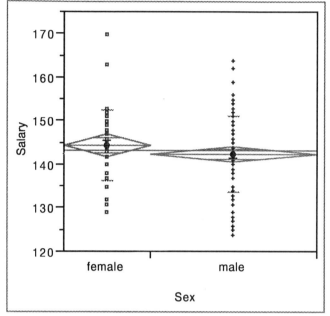

t-Test

	Difference	t-Test	DF	Prob>ltl
Estimate	2.15	1.289	114	0.2000
Std Error	1.67			
Lower 95%	-1.16			
Upper 95%	5.46			Assuming equal variances

Means

Level	Number	Mean	Std Error
female	40	144.600	1.35
male	76	142.447	0.98

Std Error uses a pooled estimate of error variance

Means and Std Deviations

Level	Number	Mean	Std Dev	Std Err Mean
female	40	144.600	8.23	1.30
male	76	142.447	8.71	1.00

Here is a side-by-side view of the two comparisons, with that on the left having all of the employees and that on the right with just showing the mid-level managers.

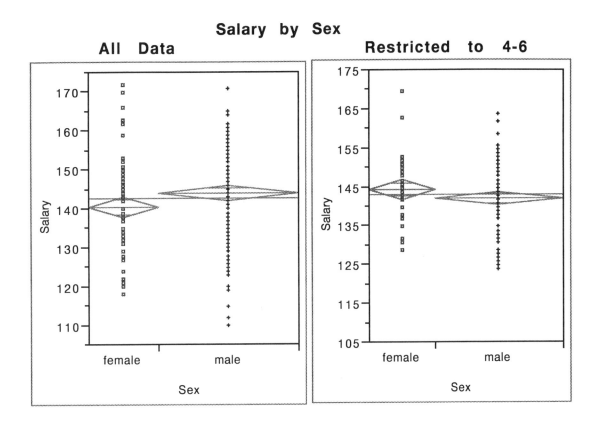

A business magazine has done a large survey that appears to indicate that mid-level female managers are being paid less than their male counterparts.

Is this claim valid?

An initial analysis using all data indicates that women in this sample are paid less, significantly so. Further analysis finds other differences between the two groups, however, such as in their level of experience and position in the firm. Restricting attention to those observations that occupy mid-level positions suggests that women are paid a bit more than their male counterparts.

The comparison limited to positions 4 to 6 restricts attention to a subset of about half of the data. Clearly, one does not want to sacrifice data, but here it perhaps makes more sense to compare similar employees than to confound differences in experience and position with sex. Later when you learn more about regression analysis, you will discover other ways to adjust for confounding effects that do not require setting aside substantial portions of the data. We will introduce regression analysis in Class 11.

Class 10. Covariance, Correlation, and Portfolios

Tests based on paired comparisons discussed in Class 8 are often able to detect differences that would require much larger samples without the pairing. Why does this pairing work?

Owners of stock often want to reduce the ups and downs of the value of their holdings — at least they want to reduce the downs! One method for reducing the risk associated with their holdings is to diversify these holdings by buying various stocks. How should the stocks for a portfolio be chosen?

The notion of covariance as a measure of dependence provides a means to answer both of these questions and provides important insights that are fundamental to regression analysis, a tool with many applications and nuances that is introduced in Class 11.

Topics

Negative and positive associations

Independent and dependent measurements

Covariance and correlation

Scatterplot matrix

Effect of dependence on the variance of an average

Risk reduction via portfolios

Example

Building a portfolio

Key Application

Constructing optimal portfolios. Simple statistical ideas underlie some of the basic theories of financial economics for which theory revolves around balancing return and risk. Risk is basically understood via the variability of returns on an asset. To construct an optimal portfolio — one that balances risk and return —you need to understand how returns on a stock are related to returns on the market. You will learn more about this topic in your finance courses, but statistics provides the background and concepts for defining how we measure the "relationship" between two variables. The appropriate measures are covariance and correlation, and these are the subject of this class.

Definitions

Covariance. A measure of strength of linear association, determined from the correlation via the relationship

$$\text{Cov}(X,Y) = \text{SD}(X)\ \text{SD}(Y)\ \text{Corr}(X,Y)\ .$$

Correlation. Strength of the linear relationship between two variables as measured on a standardized scale on which both variables share a common $\text{SD} = 1$.

Concepts

Covariance and correlation. Both describe the tendency of two quantities to move together, either over time or between sampled items. Covariance and correlation are both "two variable concepts." You would have to have at least two columns in a spreadsheet to calculate a covariance or a correlation.

Covariance and correlation are very closely related. They both tell you how two measurements vary together. Correlation measures how close a scatterplot of the two variables lies to a straight line, that is, how *linearly* related the two variables are. Covariance can be harder to interpret since it depends on the units of measurement; correlation works on a normalized scale so that its value does not depend on the units of measurement.

To be precise, the covariance between two variables, X and Y, denoted by $\text{Cov}(X,Y)$, determines the correlation $\text{Corr}(X,Y)$ via the formula

$$\text{Corr}(X,Y) = \frac{\text{Cov}(X,Y)}{\text{SD}(X)\ \text{SD}(Y)}\ ,$$

where $\text{SD}(X)$ is the standard deviation of X and $\text{SD}(Y)$ is the standard deviation of Y.

Consequently, $\text{Corr}(X,Y)$ is called "dimensionless," which is a fancy way of saying that it has no units associated with it. That means you can easily compare correlations. For example you could compare the correlation of IBM and the S&P500 with the correlation of Hitachi and the Nikkei index. You couldn't easily compare the covariances, because they retain the original scale of the measurements and the Nikkei index is measured on a very different scale from the S&P500.

To summarize, correlations are comparable but covariances are not unless the scales of the variables are similar. Which one you want to use depends on the context, but it is important to remember that you can always go from one to the other via the formula given above. They both measure the strength of a *linear relationship* but on different scales. Covariance retains the scale of the original variables but correlation does not; correlation is dimensionless. In fact, the correlation has to fall between -1 and $+1$,

$$-1 \leq \mathrm{Corr}(X,Y) \leq 1,$$

with $+1$ or -1 indicating a perfect straight-line relationship and 0 indicating no linear relationship.

Potential Confusers

No correlation $\neq$ independence. The absence of correlation does not imply the absence of any relationship between the two variables. Correlation is a standardized measure of the *strength of a linear relationship*. Linear is the operative word. It is quite possible for two variables to be highly related in a nonlinear way; for example, average cost plotted on the number of units produced in theory follows a so-called "U-shaped" or quadratic curve. The two variables are related, but not linearly. The trap you want to avoid is making a statement like "because there is no correlation, there is nothing interesting in the data."

How big does a correlation have to be before you call it large? This is a natural question to ask, but unfortunately it's almost impossible to answer. It really depends on the substantive context. What is big for someone working in finance might be no good for an engineer. The analysis of time series data is full of very high correlations (often above 0.95), whereas it can be exciting in cross-sectional social research on opinions and consumer attitudes to see a correlation of 0.25.

Stocks, Portfolios, and the Efficient Frontier

FinMark.jmp, StockRet.jmp, Frontier.jmp, Portfol.xls

Historically, it's "well known" that the stock market has outperformed other investments. It also seems well known that the stock market moves up and down, so that the value of stocks as an investment, unlike a savings account, can go up or down from one day to the next.

Is it true that the stock market outperforms safer, "risk-free" investments like U.S. Treasury bills? If so, how does one avoid the risks of sudden changes in the direction of the market to reap the gains of these long-term trends?

Three data sets and a spreadsheet are used in this example. The time series used in preparing this handout were extracted from the CRSP data files with the help of Craig MacKinley of the Wharton Finance Department. Dave Hildebrand created the initial Excel spreadsheet. We greatly appreciate their help. Each time series is aggregated to a monthly scale. The files are

(1) *FinMark.jmp*: Monthly long-term indices (1926–1994) that track the value of investments in the stock market and 3-month Treasury bills (T-bills). The stock market's overall performance is tracked by the "value-weighted index," which assumes that one buys all stocks in the market in proportion to their capitalized value (i.e., you buy more of the big ones, fewer of the small ones).

The indices are scaled so that the value of each is 100 in January 1973. The data set also includes the U.S. Consumer Price Index (CPI) so that we can see whether there is any risk in holding these investments.

(2) *StockRet.jmp*: Monthly returns on the indices from FinMark.jmp as well as returns on a collection of 24 other stocks for the 20 year period from 1975 to 1994.

(3) *Frontier.jmp*: Average return and variance of different types of portfolios constructed from the stocks in StockRet.jmp.

(4) *Portfol.xls:* This small Excel 5 spreadsheet shows how to use the "Solver" tool to find the optimal portfolio from a collection of six stocks featured in our analysis.

As noted in the opening question, long-term trends favor stocks as an investment over T-bills. Although stocks move up or down in value, the following plots show that, in general, they clearly outperform T-bills.

The two indices shown in the overlay plot below are matched at 100 in 1973. Thus, you can interpret the value of either index as the amount of money that you would need to have had in either the market or T-bills in order for the investment to be worth $100 in January 1973 (highlighted by the reference horizontal line in the figure).

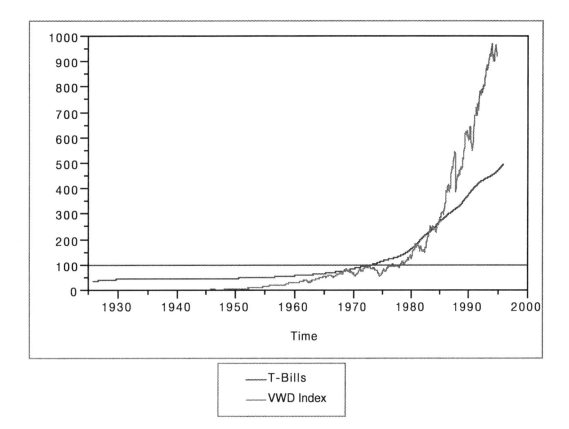

The scale of the plot makes it hard to see what is happening in the years prior to 1970. As we saw with executive compensation, most of the data values are small compared to the relatively few large values.

Moving to a log scale improves the appearance of the plot and reveals a consistent upward trend in the value of the market. The "roughness" of the market's growth also suggests some of the inherent "volatility" in this investment.

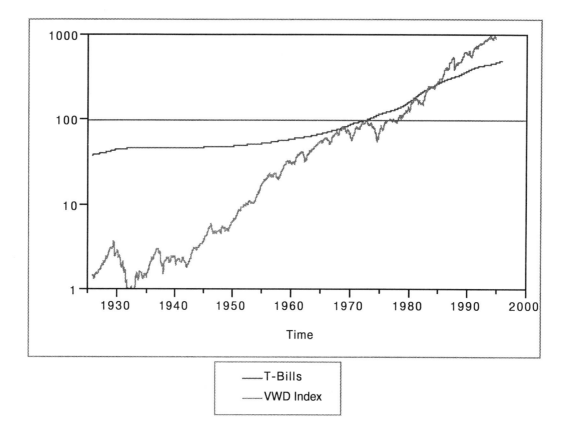

The linearity of the growth of the market on the log scale shown here implies that its value has grown exponentially. We'll study such trends much more in Statistics 621, but notice that exponential growth on the original scale implies linear growth on a logarithmic scale:

Exponential growth $V_t = k\, e^t \Rightarrow$ Linear growth $\log V_t = \log k + t$,

Some of the gains in these indices can be attributed to inflation. Adding the Consumer Price Index to the plot changes your impression of the lack of risk in the "risk-free" T-bills. The second plot shows the difference of the T-bill index minus the CPI.

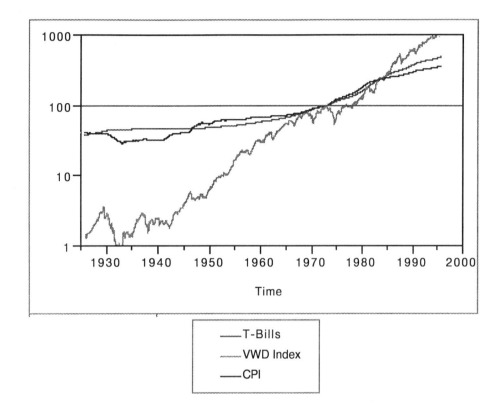

Until recently, T-bills have often returned less than inflation has taken away.

Plot

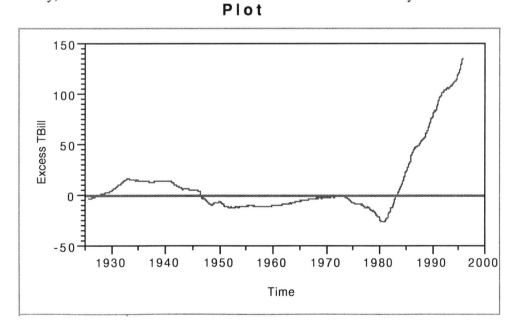

Rather than look at further time trends, the plot below compares the returns defined as in prior examples as

$$R_t = \frac{V_t - V_{t-1}}{V_{t-1}} \quad .$$

The conversion to monthly returns eliminates the trends in the indices and highlights something hidden in the time series plots: the volatility of the stock market index. Returns on the market have been much more variable than returns on T-bills.

This plot also helps you appreciate just how volatile the market was during the 1930s during the Great Depression. Monthly changes in this stock index of ±10% – 20% were common. It's as though the market behaved as it did recently in October 1987, but did so with unsettling regularity.

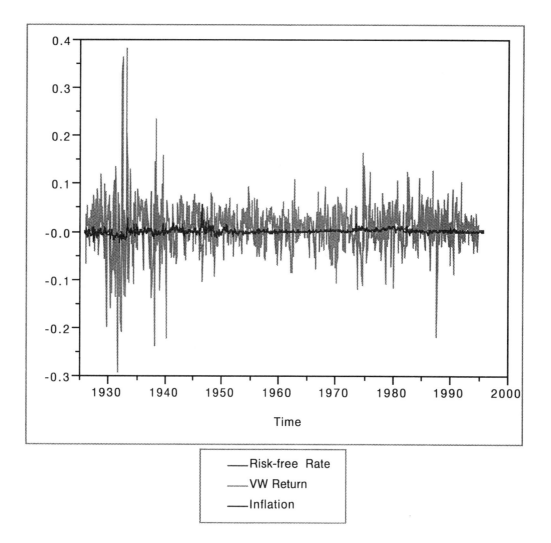

Since the returns show little trend over this time span, we can safely compress the data into histograms. ("Little trend" is a relative expression; fortunes have been made exploiting what little trend there is.) The histograms shown below share a common scale. Over the years 1926 to 1994, the average monthly return on T-bills is about 0.3% — roughly an annual rate of 3.6%. Inflation has averaged about 3.12%, so the return on the T-bills has only been about 0.5% above the rate of inflation.

In comparison, the return on the market has averaged about 11.28% for an excess return of 8% over the CPI. The return on the market has also been much more variable.

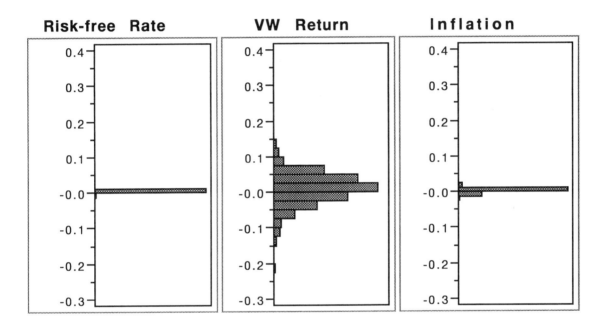

Moments

	Risk-free Rate	VW Return	Inflation
Mean	0.0030	0.0094	0.0026
Std Dev	0.0027	0.0555	0.0056
Std Error Mean	0.0001	0.0019	0.0002
Upper 95% Mean	0.0032	0.0132	0.0030
Lower 95% Mean	0.0029	0.0056	0.0022
N	840	827	840

For the rest of this example, we will focus on the 20-year period spanning January 1975 through December 1994. The plot below focuses on the returns from the data file StockRet.jmp. Once again, the returns show relatively little trend, with those of the market being much more volatile than those associated with owning T-bills. Histograms of the associated returns follow on the next page.

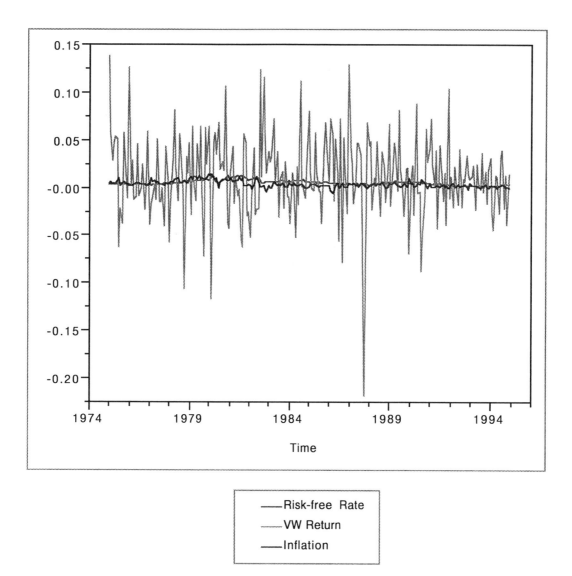

During these 20 years, the average monthly return on the market has been about 1.25%, roughly annualized to $12 \times 1.25 = 15\%$. In comparison, T-bills returned about 7% with inflation averaging 5.3% per year. The histogram of the returns on the market makes it clear that although its average is positive, its month-to-month change is highly variable.

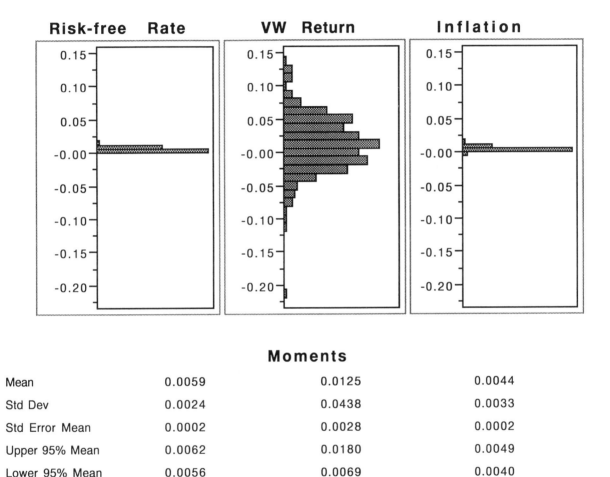

Moments

	Risk-free Rate	VW Return	Inflation
Mean	0.0059	0.0125	0.0044
Std Dev	0.0024	0.0438	0.0033
Std Error Mean	0.0002	0.0028	0.0002
Upper 95% Mean	0.0062	0.0180	0.0049
Lower 95% Mean	0.0056	0.0069	0.0040
N	240	240	240

In spite of the outliers associated with October 1987 (use the column *Date* as a point label), the distribution of the monthly returns on the market approximates normality reasonably well. The data is a bit "fat-tailed," with observations drifting away from normality at the extremes. This behavior is common in financial data and has been extensively discussed in the literature.

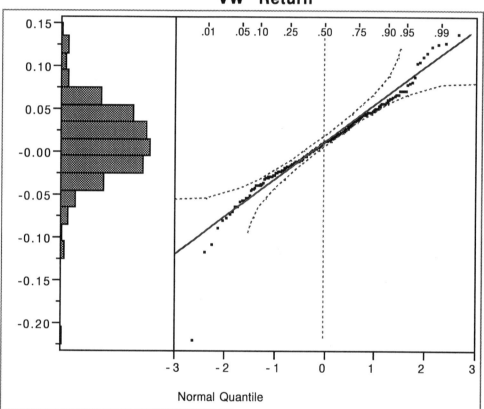

In addition to these broad indices, the data file StockRet.jmp includes the monthly returns (adjusted for dividends and splits) for 24 individual stocks. These stocks were chosen based on their capitalized value in 1974. We selected "big" stocks from several industries, including retail, oil, finance, and manufacturing. Some of our initial companies (11 out of 35) did not "survive" for the full 20 years, and we set those aside. Consequently, the range of choices here is a bit "optimistic" since all 24 companies have lasted for the full 20 years. All of the portfolios we will be considering are built from the stocks of companies that survived the full period. In reality, one might not expect all of the stocks in a portfolio to last so long. Some companies will fold, and others will be bought or merged with others.

Put yourself now in the place of an investment consultant who, in January 1975, is charged with forming a stock portfolio for a client. A stock portfolio is an investment made up of several stocks. For example, looking forward from 1975, you might want to focus on retail stocks. The next page shops how two retail stocks, those of Sears and J.C. Penney, performed over the years 1975 to 1994. Not only do both of these on average under perform the market, each stock is also more variable than the overall market. Neither in retrospect is a good choice, but then who knew that in 1974?

To reduce the total variability of an investment in stocks, one generally buys several stocks. For example, the values on the right-hand side of the next page show the performance of a portfolio in which the investor equally split the investment into Sears and Penney,

$$\frac{Sears + Penney}{2} \ .$$

The investor who purchases this evenly balanced mix of the two gets the average level of performance. However, the investor also gets *slightly less volatility*; the SD of the portfolio made from these two is smaller than that of either single stock.

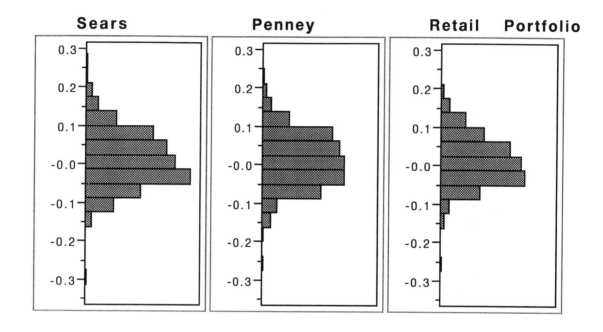

Moments

Mean	**0.0116**	**0.0118**	**0.0117**
Std Dev	**0.0745**	**0.0714**	**0.0658**
Std Error Mean	0.0048	0.0046	0.0043
Upper 95% Mean	0.0211	0.0209	0.0201
Lower 95% Mean	0.0022	0.0027	0.0033
N	240	240	240

A more "fortunate" investment consultant might have chosen the oil industry, looking for a big recovery after the "energy crisis" of the early 1970s that accompanied the first oil embargo of 1973. Individually, these stocks generally outperformed the market (the market's average monthly return is 0.0125). But again, each stock is more variable than the market (the market's SD is 0.044).

Again, the associated portfolio of equal parts of these two obtains the average rate of return and has slightly less volatility than Amoco. The portfolio has higher variance than Exxon since Amoco was rather volatile during these years. (Don't you wish you loaded up on Exxon stock in 1975? Hindsight investments are always more easy that those looking forward!)

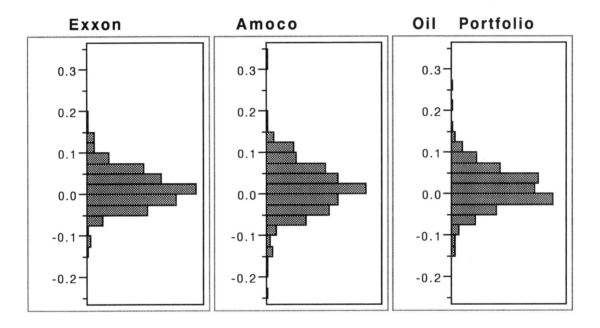

Moments

	Exxon	Amoco	Oil Portfolio
Mean	0.0147	0.0142	0.0144
Std Dev	0.0480	0.0666	0.0523
Std Error Mean	0.0031	0.0043	0.0034
Upper 95% Mean	0.0208	0.0227	0.0211
Lower 95% Mean	0.0086	0.0057	0.0078
N	240	240	240

Each of the prior two portfolios combines two stocks from the same industry, retail or oil. Such strategies work well, in the sense of high returns, when the choice of the industry is a good one (oil), but they don't work so well when you pick the wrong industry (retail). Neither does much to reduce variation. Consequently, many investors might prefer to spread their investment dollars over different companies in different industries, such as combining, say, GM with J.P. Morgan.

Once again, the portfolio of equal parts of these stocks obtains the average monthly return, but in this case the *drop in variation is much more marked* than in the prior two examples. The advantage of mixing stocks from different industries is that by spreading our investment over two segments of the economy, we gain much less month-to-month variation.

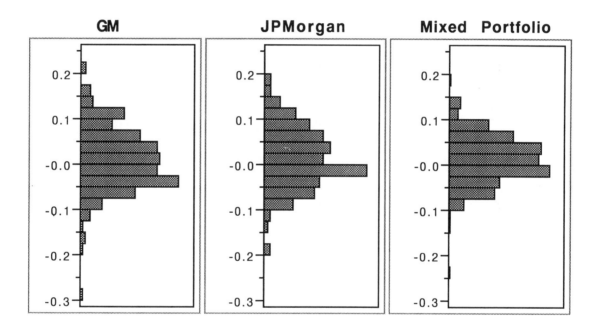

Moments

	GM	JPMorgan	Mixed Portfolio
Mean	0.0102	0.0136	0.0119
Std Dev	0.0705	0.0686	0.0545
Std Error Mean	0.0045	0.0044	0.0035
Upper 95% Mean	0.0192	0.0224	0.0189
Lower 95% Mean	0.0013	0.0049	0.0050
N	240	240	240

Covariance and correlation explain the logic of combining stocks from different industries and lead to a precise way of building an "optimal" portfolio. Returns on stocks from the retail industry are highly related, as measured by the *correlation*. The scatterplot matrix shown below depicts the correlation graphically. (The scatterplot matrix is much more useful when looking at more than two variables, but it's conveniently generated from the output of the *Correlation of Y's* tool. Again, using the *Date* variable for point labels is useful for identifying outliers.)

Correlations

Variable	Sears	Penney
Sears	1.000	0.631
Penney	0.631	1.000

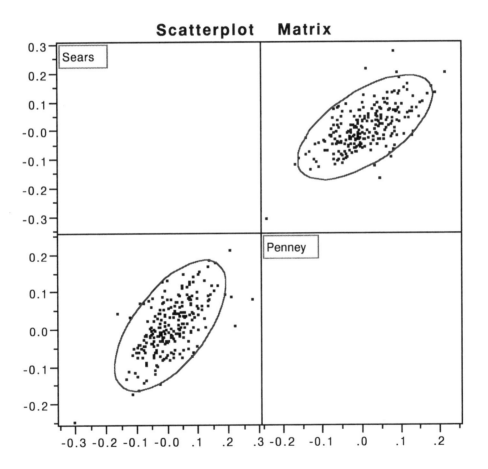

One obtains a similar correlation for the returns in the oil industry. These high correlations among the stocks cause a problem when we try to make a portfolio. The obvious risk of "putting all our eggs in one basket" shows up in the variation of the associated portfolio. Put simply, combining correlated stocks in a portfolio does little to reduce the volatility of the separate stocks as investments.

Correlations

Variable	Exxon	Amoco
Exxon	1.000	0.660
Amoco	0.660	1.000

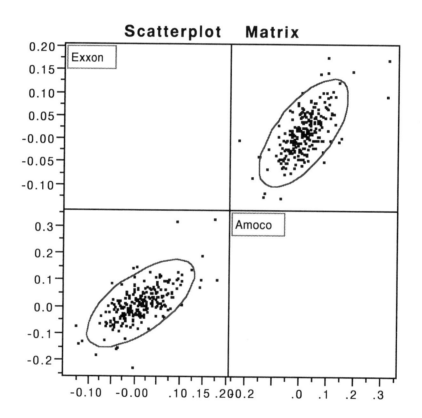

As you might expect by now, the returns of the stocks of GM and J.P. Morgan are not so related, and thus the portfolio has relatively less variation than either of the components. The diminished correlations for the returns of these two stocks appear as more circular, fatter ellipses in the associated scatterplot matrix.

Correlations

Variable	GM	JPMorgan
GM	1.000	0.229
JPMorgan	0.229	1.000

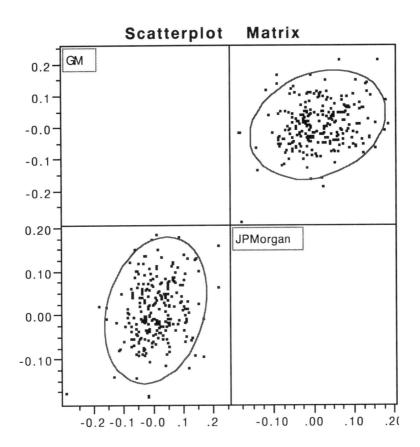

In order to see how correlation affects the variation of a portfolio, we have to change from correlations (which do not depend on the scale of measurement) to covariances which do. The covariance of two variables (columns) is

$$Cov(X,Y) = SD(X) \ SD(Y) \ Corr(X,Y) \ .$$

For example, the covariance matrix for the retail stocks is as follows (computed by hand using SD(*Sears*) = 0.0745 and SD(*Penney*) = 0.0714), with variances along the diagonal.

Covariance Matrix

Variable	Sears	Penney
Sears	.0056	.0034
Penney	.0034	.0051

Covariance is more useful than correlation in this context because it shows how the variance of the portfolio depends on the variances and covariances of the stocks that constitute the portfolio. In general, with weights w_1 and w_2, we have

$$\text{Variance } (w_1 Sears + w_2 Penney)$$
$$= w_1^2 \ Var(Sears) + w_2^2 \ Var(Penney) + 2 \ w_1 w_2 \ Cov(Sears, Penney) \ .$$

With equal weights $w_1 = w_2 = 1/2$ as in the example, the variance of the portfolio is

$$\begin{aligned}
Var(1/2 \ Sears + 1/2 \ Penney) \\
= 1/4 \ Var(Sears) + 1/4 \ Var(Penney) + 1/2 \ Cov(Sears, Penney) \\
= 1/4 \ 0.0056 + 1/4 \ 0.0051 + 1/2 \ 0.0034 \\
= 0.0014 + 0.0013 + \ 0.0017 \\
= 0.0044,
\end{aligned}$$

so that the $SD = \sqrt{Var} = \sqrt{0.0044} = 0.066$, within rounding error of the SD computed for the retail portfolio earlier.

Notice how the covariance shows up in the expression for the variance of the portfolio. Were the two stocks *uncorrelated*, then their covariance would also be zero and the variance of the portfolio would be only 0.0027. *The larger the covariance among the returns, the larger the variance of the associated portfolio.*

More generally, stock portfolios are made by combining many more than two or three companies. The file Optimal.jmp holds the average return and variance of the return for portfolios comprised in different ways from the stocks in this example. Some of these portfolios will have negative weights. These negative weights correspond to *short selling* a stock. In effect, short selling a stock implies that you suspect its value will go down in the future rather than increase. Short selling allows one to profit not only by investing in stocks whose value you suspect will rise, but also by "betting against" others that you think will decline. In each case, the sum of the weights in the portfolio is 1, indicating how we want to invest each $1 in the market.

To begin, here is a plot of the return on the variance for each stock. In general (though there is clearly a lot of variation), the larger the variance of the stock, the higher the return.

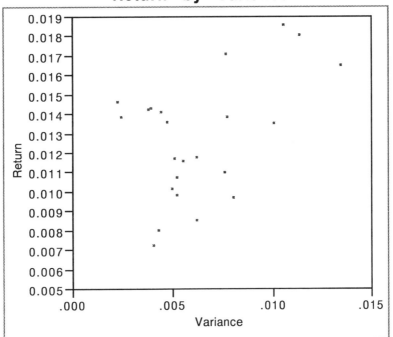

In the next plot, we've added the average return and variance of portfolios based on an equally weighted mixture of two (top) and three (bottom) randomly chosen stocks. Notice how the variances of these cluster on the left of the figure. Mixing stocks reduces the variance of the portfolio.

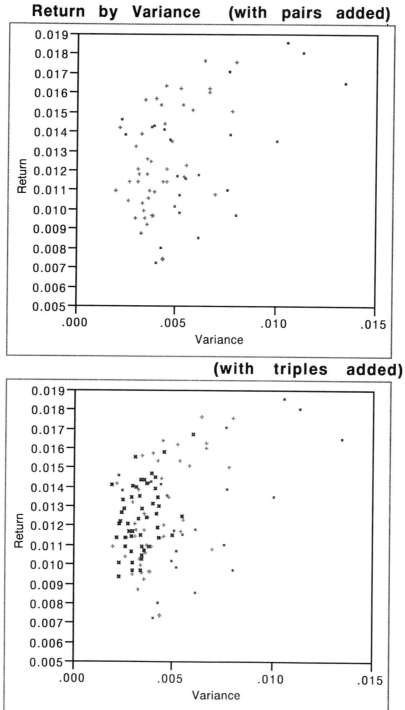

To this point, we have forced our portfolios to be equally weighted. One gets a wider range of possibilities by allowing not only different weights (such as $2/3$ and $1/3$) but also negative weights ("shorting" stocks).

The figure below adds the performance of simple portfolios of two stocks, but with weights 2 and –1. How can we put a weight greater than 1 on any given stock? The answer is that we "sell" someone else shares of stocks. The trick is that we sell them shares of stocks we do not own. We then take the money from this sale and invest it in our own portfolio. This so-called short selling lets us invest more heavily in a stock we like. We can lose as well, for if the stock that we "sold" to someone else rises in value, we are going to lose money since in the end we'll need to purchase it on the market at the higher price than we "sold" it previously.

This flexibility leads to much more variation, and occasionally much higher returns as well. The portfolios with the very high returns are also the portfolios with very high volatility.

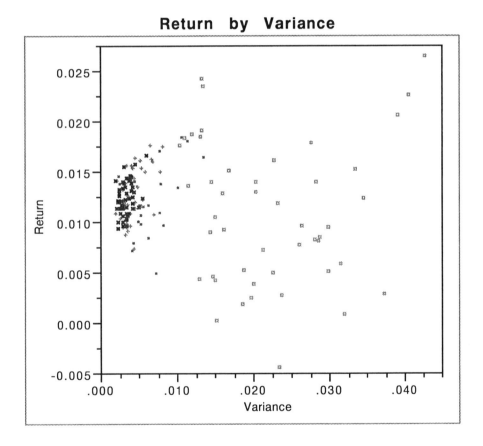

Finally, the plot below shows a richer set of portfolios, mixing many more stocks with a bit of clever strategy which reveals the "efficient frontier," the quadratic boundary on the edge of the points shown.

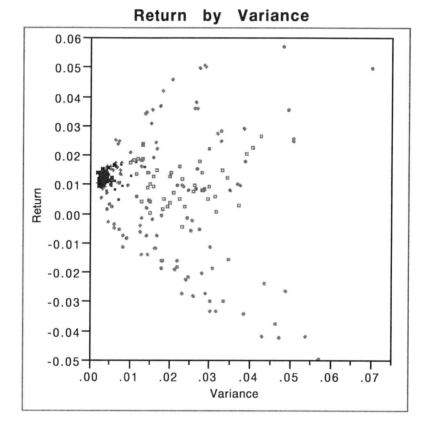

Such "dart throwing" is not a particularly good way to find the optimal portfolio in this problem. In fact, given your willingness to accept volatility (risk, variance), there is just one optimal portfolio. Given a level of variation, it is a fairly simple task to determine the optimal portfolio. It's tedious, though, so we'll use Excel for the details.

The Excel spreadsheet Portfol.xls shows how you can use the built-in "Solver" tool to find the optimal portfolio. The example uses just the 6 stocks that we have been considering, not the larger collection of 24 in the stock returns data file.

When you open this spreadsheet, the cells will be filled with the values seen below. The means and SDs in the first two rows come directly from the previous JMP output, and the correlations were also pasted in from JMP. (You can cut and paste pretty easily by copying the JMP correlation matrix as text and then pasting it into Excel.) The line of weights shown below the correlations describes a portfolio that shorts Sears and GM and loads up on Exxon. Below the weights, we see that this portfolio attains a monthly return of about 1.6% with SD = 0.0545, the same SD as the mixed portfolio constructed before. Although it has the same level of risk as our simple mixed portfolio, this new portfolio has much higher return. The mixed portfolio of GM and J.P. Morgan returned about 1.2%. Our new portfolio, in fact, has the highest return of any portfolio constructed from these six stocks with this level of risk (SD = 0.0545).

Means	0.011641	0.011775	0.014674	0.014187	0.010219	0.01364
Std.Devs.	0.074461	0.071386	0.047958	0.066625	0.070483	0.068649

Correlations

Stock	Sears	Penney	Exxon	Amoco	GM	JPMorgan
Sears	1	0.6307	0.306	0.19	0.5463	0.4239
Penney	0.6307	1	0.122	-0.0045	0.4999	0.4042
Exxon	0.306	0.122	1	0.6598	0.2827	0.4208
Amoco	0.19	-0.0045	0.6598	1	0.1404	0.156
GM	0.5463	0.4999	0.2827	0.1404	1	0.2288
JPMorgan	0.4239	0.4042	0.4208	0.156	0.2288	1

Weights	-0.12477	0.264289	1.146936	-0.00964	-0.3398	0.062993

Portfolio Mean	0.01574
Portfolio Variance	0.00297
Portfolio Std. Dev.	0.0545

How did we find this portfolio? The important formulas underlie the values in lines 15 and 16 of column B, which are labeled "Portfolio Mean" and "Portfolio Variance." These use some of Excel's "array formulas" to compute the average and variance of a portfolio formed from these six stocks using the weights shown in the row labeled "Weights." You can use these formulas with a bigger correlation matrix based on more stocks to explore other portfolios.

The Excel Solver tool finds the weights that maximize the return given a stated level of risk (here, in terms of the SD of the portfolio). Choosing the *Solver...* item from the Excel *Tools* menu opens a dialog that allows you to find the optimal portfolio by varying the stock weights. The dialog is initially configured to find the portfolio with the maximum return while constraining the SD to be no larger than 0.0545 and the weights summing to 1. You can change these constraints to explore other solutions. For example, as you increase the acceptable level of risk, you will see a higher return. If you increase the acceptable SD to 0.10, then the maximum possible return climbs to 1.9%. The portfolio weights also change, indicating the need for more short selling to attain this level of return:

Stock	Sears	Penney	Exxon	Amoco	GM	JPMorgan
Weights	-0.23716	0.321294	2.147181	-0.2101	-1.04191	0.020696

If you vary the weights and keep track of the variance and the return, you'll see that the values of the mean return plotted on the variance trace out a quadratic curve that you'll more about in finance courses, the efficient frontier.

Historically, it's "well known" that the stock market has outperformed other investments. It also seems well known that the stock market moves up and down, so that the value of stocks as an investment, unlike a savings account, can go up or down from one day to the next.

Is it true that the stock market outperforms safer, "risk-free" investments like U.S. Treasury bills? If so, how does one avoid the risks of sudden changes in the direction of the market to reap the gains of these long-term trends?

Over the long haul, stocks have shown higher average returns than T-bills. T-bills, a so-called risk-free asset, are perhaps not so risk-free. During some periods, inflation exceeded the interest rate on T-bills, so that holding T-bills was a poor investment. Portfolios reduce the variability of the investments in the stock market while keeping the average return of the included stocks. More advanced methods explore the efficient frontier, seeking portfolios that maximize the return for a given level of risk.

An aside on paired comparisons:

Covariance also explains the "success" of paired comparisons in finding differences between means that would be missed in the comparable two-sample analysis. The success of the paired t-test comes from the fact that the two samples of measurements are correlated. This correlation leads to a smaller standard error for the comparison of the two means.

In our discussion of the variance of a portfolio, we introduced the important formula that says, in general, that the variance of a weighted sum of two stocks S_1 and S_2 is

$$\text{Var}\,(w_1\,S_1 + w_2\,S_2) = (w_1)^2\,\text{Var}(S_1) + (w_2)^2\,\text{Var}(S_2) + 2\,w_1\,w_2\,\text{Cov}(S_1, S_2)\,.$$

This formula works just as well with sample means as it does with stocks, implying that

$$\text{Var}\,(w_1\,\overline{X}_1 + w_2\,\overline{X}_2) = (w_1)^2\,\text{Var}(\overline{X}_1) + (w_2)^2\,\text{Var}(\overline{X}_2) + 2\,w_1\,w_2\,\text{Cov}(\overline{X}_1, \overline{X}_2)\,.$$

Usually, we don't need this very general expression, just the special case for the difference with $w_1 = 1$, $w_2 = -1$,

$$\text{Var}\,(\overline{X}_1 - \overline{X}_2) = \text{Var}(\overline{X}_1) + \text{Var}(\overline{X}_2) - 2\,\text{Cov}(\overline{X}_1, \overline{X}_2)\,.$$

Notice what happens when the two means are positively correlated: positive correlation means that the covariance is positive, and thus the variance of the difference in the means is smaller than it would have been were the two samples (and means) independent of one another. A bit more algebra leads to the formula (assuming equal variance in the two groups each of size n with correlation ρ):

$$\text{Var}(\overline{X}_1 - \overline{X}_2) = \frac{2\sigma^2}{n}\,(1-\rho)$$

This formula means that we would need $n/(1-\rho)$ observations in each of two independent samples to do just as well (same length CI for the difference) as we can with n paired, correlated observations.

Class 11. A Preview of Regression

This final class reviews ideas covered in the first 10 lectures, and introduces the methods that will be covered in courses that deal with regression analysis. In particular, we consider how to fit regression lines that model the dependence between two variables. An underlying theme is the importance of the assumption of independence.

Huge numbers of people spend large amounts of time analyzing and tracking financial data. Their hope is that by understanding the nature and structure of past data they will be in a better position to make shrewd investment decisions for the future. This view rests solidly on the notion that the future looks something like the past. If it didn't then there wouldn't be any point in looking at the historical data. What does it mean to believe and how do we operationalize the idea of the future "looking like the past?" One way is to assert that the variables in which we are interested follow, at least on the average, some regular pattern, and that this pattern should continue into the future. To be more specific, consider the relationship between the threat or outbreak of war in the Middle East and the spot price of crude oil. There is a *past* pattern and it does seem reasonable to believe that this will hold into the *future*.

We can take this idea of looking for a pattern, relationship or association much further. In fact, we often analyze data to see if such a pattern exists, in the hope that we can exploit it if we find it. Pattern is not exactly a well defined term — most often we look for a pattern after assuming that it takes a certain form. The most simple (and useful) one to look for is a straight line and it's here that we start the beginning of a large subject called "linear regression."

Topics
    Correlation and linear regression.
    Dependence and p-values.

Example
    Performance of mutual funds

Key Application

Mutual funds. Many billions of dollars were invested in mutual funds in 1996. Mutual funds are popular with small as well as institutional investors, and a large number of companies offer advice on just where to invest your money. Their advice, unless purely of an astrological nature, relies heavily on the belief that by looking at past performance and current trends convey some inkling of what is going to happen in the future. Indeed, one of the common boasts of a successful mutual fund is that it was a consistent top performer over a recent past period. In today's example we will examine the extent a fund's past performance is an indicator of its future gains.

Overview

Assuming that there might be a relationship between past and future performance of mutual funds, we want to specify it. To make matters more concrete, consider two "variables" — the percentage return on investments in a mutual fund in 1990 and percentage return in 1991. The advertising claims of some funds suggest that a fund's return in 1990 gives you some information about what will happen in 1991, at least "on average." One way of making such a claim precise is to express it through what we call a "model." Here, a simple model might state that

Average returns in 1991 depends upon the return in 1990 in a linear fashion.

In a mathematical notation we can express this claim as the linear equation

$$\text{Average(Return 1991} \mid \text{Return 1990)} = \beta_0 + \beta_1 \text{ Return1990}.$$

This equation (the model) indicates that we believe the average return in 1991 depends on the return in 1990, and that the relationship is linear, along a straight line. It is quite likely that if you have not seen such an equation before, this one does not look like the typical equation for a straight line that you would have seen in a math class, but it is! It's got a slope, β_1, and an intercept β_0. For the generic situation, we have a predictor variable called X, and a response variable called Y, so X tries to predict the response Y. Using these symbols, the model is

$$\text{Average}(Y \mid X) = \beta_0 + \beta_1 X.$$

In this model, the slope and the intercept are not known; all that the model asserts is that the relationship is a straight line. Just as we have used sample data to estimate the population mean μ using the sample mean $\overline{X}$, we will use the data itself to get best estimates for β_0 and β_1. Technically, the slope and intercept are unknown population parameters (which is why they have been denoted by Greek letters). In practice, the data is used to obtain "sample estimates" which we will denote as b_0 and b_1.

Class 10 looked at the idea of correlation, a measure of a linear relationship. Since the first model that we have seen is a "straight line model" it should come as no surprise to learn that the two are connected. In fact correlation measures precisely how well a straight line model actually fits the data.

Definition

Linear regression. A statistical model that states that the average value of one variable, known as the "response" and denoted by the symbol Y, varies linearly with changes in another variable, known as the "predictor" and denoted X.

Potential Confuser

Why specify a model for the average value of Y and not for Y itself?

In truth, the response Y depends on more than just a single predictor X. Typically Y is made up of two parts. One part depends on the value of X, and the other part is comprised of pure noise or variability. That is, we think of Y as being decomposed into "signal + noise." The signal is that part of the variation in Y that can be "explained" using X. The rest is left to the noise term, with an assumption that on average the noise is zero. Hence, on average, Y is just the signal, giving a much cleaner representation to work with it.

Later, if you do more regression analysis, you will see a statistical model for plain Y itself, no longer averaged. This later regression model combines the straight line model you see above with an explicit noise term added back in.

Performance of Mutual Funds

MutFunds.jmp

Investors are often impressed by the track record of a mutual fund. How well does the track record predict performance?

The data used in this example are the annual returns of over 1500 mutual funds during the six years from 1988 to 1993. We start with a look at the returns one year at a time, and then we consider how well one can predict the return one year from the value in the preceding year. As you might expect, the returns are sometimes skewed and have outliers.

In 1993 the returns are skewed toward positive values. Note that the highest return (though not seen in the plot) is a remarkable 270%; the median return was over 12%.

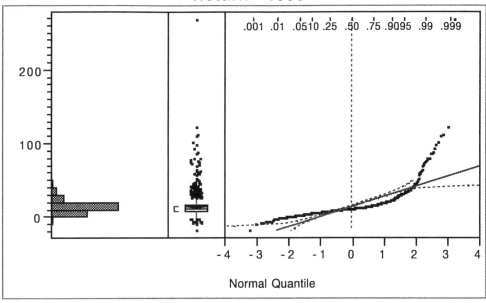

Return   1993

Quantiles

maximum	100.0%	269.78
quartile	75.0%	16.48
median	50.0%	12.31
quartile	25.0%	9.16
minimum	0.0%	-17.73

Moments

Mean	14.859
Std Dev	13.678
Std Err Mean	0.349
upper 95% Mean	15.545
lower 95% Mean	14.174
N	1533

Looking back one year to 1992, more typically, the data are approximately centered at zero, with "long tails" extending in both directions away from the center of the data. The largest return was about 60%, and the median return was near 8%.

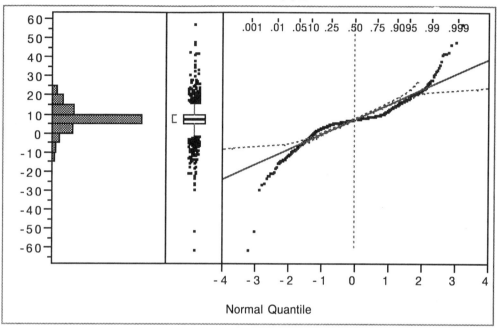

Quantiles

maximum	100.0%	57.830
quartile	75.0%	9.965
median	50.0%	7.940
quartile	25.0%	5.530
minimum	0.0%	-60.710

Moments

Mean	7.692
Std Dev	7.901
Std Err Mean	0.202
upper 95% Mean	8.088
lower 95% Mean	7.296
N	1533

Averaged over the five years prior to 1993, the returns are still skewed (what happened to the central limit theorem?). The median return was about 11%. One fund lost on average about 20%, but survived the six years. Is this collection of returns representative, since we only have those that lasted all six years?

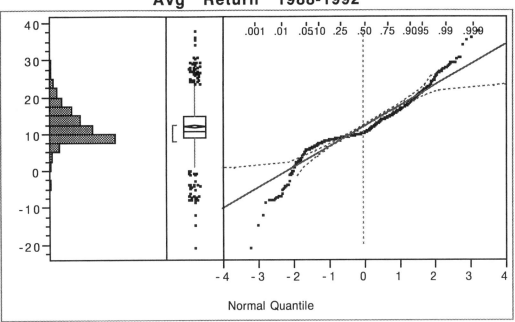

Quantiles

maximum	100.0%	38.006
quartile	75.0%	14.939
median	50.0%	10.728
quartile	25.0%	9.222
minimum	0.0%	-20.760

Moments

Mean	12.125
Std Dev	5.540
Std Err Mean	0.141
upper 95% Mean	12.403
lower 95% Mean	11.848
N	1533

It remains to be seen how well such performance tracks. Was the fund that returned 270% in 1993 also the winner in 1992? We can get a hint that such is not the case by using plot brushing in the histograms of 1992 and 1993. By selecting the lowest group in 1993 we can see that these performed about average in 1992.

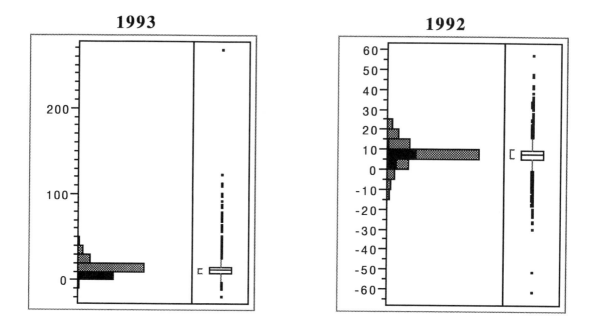

Scatterplot shown on the next page offer a more direct view of the relationship between returns in two years. It is particularly fun in these plots to look at the plot labels revealed by selecting funds. Neither the performance in the prior year nor the average return over the prior five years appears to be very closely related to the return in 1993.

Return 1993 by Return 1992

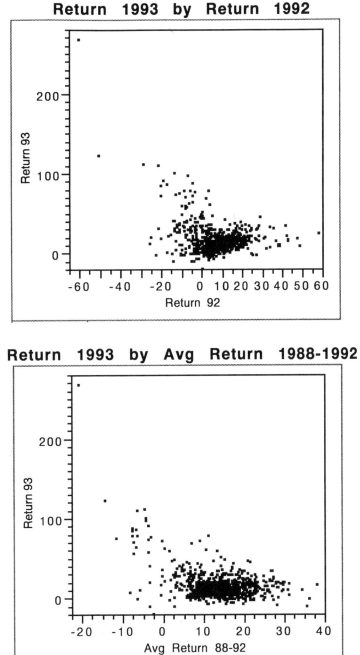

Return 1993 by Avg Return 1988-1992

It is visually apparent that there is not much association between the returns seen in the prior two scatterplots. The correlation coefficient summarizes the strength of *linear* association. Some of the correlations are positive, but more are negative.

Correlations

Variable	Return 93	Return 92	Return 91	Return 90	Return 89	Return 88
Return 93	1.0000	-0.2835	-0.1078	-0.4841	0.1804	-0.1784
Return 92	-0.2835	1.0000	0.2553	-0.0249	-0.2073	0.4143
Return 91	-0.1078	0.2553	1.0000	-0.3102	0.4144	0.3041
Return 90	-0.4841	-0.0249	-0.3102	1.0000	-0.2876	-0.2459
Return 89	0.1804	-0.2073	0.4144	-0.2876	1.0000	0.1944
Return 88	-0.1784	0.4143	0.3041	-0.2459	0.1944	1.0000

Associated with each correlation is a regression line. The fitted line for the return in 1993 regressed on that from 1992 has negative slope.

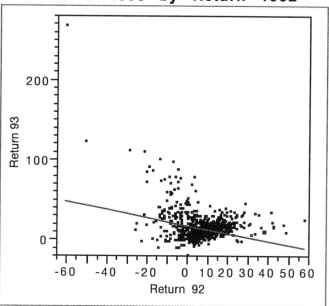

Return 1993 by Return 1992

Parameter Estimates

Term	Estimate	Std Error	Ratio	Prob>|t|
Intercept	18.634	0.4678	39.83	0.0000
Return 92	-0.49119	0.0424	-11.57	0.0000

A similar fit applies to predicting the return in 1993 from the average in the five prior years.

Return 1993 by Avg Return 1988-1992

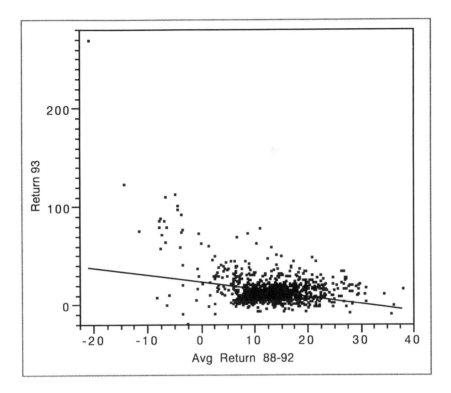

Parameter Estimates

Term	Estimate	Std Error	t Ratio	Prob>ltl
Intercept	23.669	0.803893	29.44	0.0000
Avg Return 88-92	-0.727	0.060307	-12.05	0.0000

Investors are often impressed by the track record of a mutual fund. How well does the track record predict performance?

Like it says in the small print, historical data are of little use in predicting the returns of mutual funds in 1993.

Here's supplemental question to think about: All of the funds considered in this data set have complete data over the six years of the analysis, 1988–1993. How might this attribute affect the conclusions of our analysis, and how would you try to find out?

A comment on outliers is in order in this example. Skimming the correlation matrix, we see that the largest (in absolute value) correlation is that between 1993 and 1990. From this correlation, 1990 looks like a good predictor of 1993, at least compared to 1992. A closer look suggests that correlations alone can be misleading. A relatively small subset (about 30 funds) dominates the slope calculation. Since the analysis covers 1533 funds, the outliers are about 2% of the data.

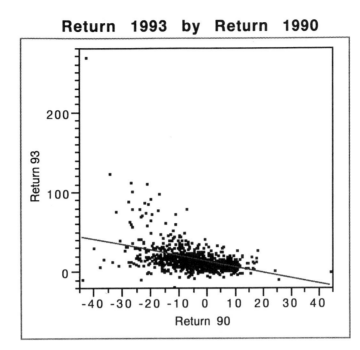

Parameter Estimates

Term	Estimate	Std Error	t Ratio	Prob>|t|
Intercept	14.1674	0.307	46.08	0.0000
Return 90	-0.6917	0.032	-21.65	0.0000

Setting these influential few aside (use the *Exclude* command on the *Rows* menu) the slope is about half of the former size, dropping in magnitude from about –0.69 to –0.39. Both fitted lines appear in the next plot.

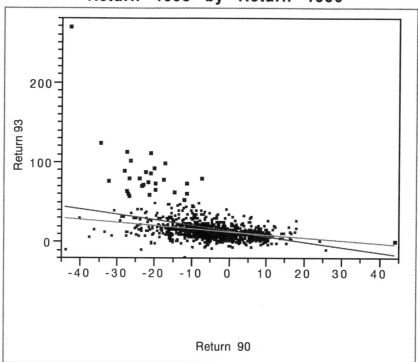

Return 1993 by Return 1990

Parameter Estimates Using All 1533 Funds

Term	Estimate	Std Error	t Ratio	Prob>|t|
Intercept	14.167422	0.307461	46.08	0.0000
Return 90	-0.**69171**	0.031957	-21.65	0.0000

Parameter Estimates Using 1504 Funds

Term	Estimate	Std Error	t Ratio	Prob>|t|
Intercept	13.285049	0.185455	71.63	0.0000
Return 90	-0.**387672**	0.020377	-19.02	0.0000

Assignments

Assignment 0

Create a new JMP data file (use the *New* command from the *File* menu) with the following information on the R&D expenses (as a percentage of profits) of 33 chemical firms as reported in *Business Week*, June 29, 1992. Use the *Add Rows* command from the *Rows* menu to create the needed 33 empty rows; if you decide to enter the company names, the column that holds them must be defined to be a character column. The data are as follows:

Company	R&D Expense
Air Products	22.2
Amer Cyanamid	90.8
Arco	20.1
Betz	21.6
Cabot	53.1
Crompton	17.1
Dexter	375.8
Dow	68.7
DuPont	46.1
Englehard	38.3
Ethly	23.5
F&C Intl	85.9
Ferro	82.1
First Mississippi	50.0
Fuller	36.3
GI Holdings	8.9
Grace	41.9
Great Lakes	12.2
Hercules	52.0
Intl Specialty	22.5
Lawter	10.7
LeaRonal	21.6
Loctite	23.5
Lubrizol	44.9
MacDermid	55.8
Monsanto	136.9
Morton Intl	27.3
Nalco Chem	21.4
Petrolite	51.1
Rohm & Haas	76.3
Scotts	114.9
Trans Resources	14.1
Witco	25.4

Hand in a printed copy of the histogram and boxplot computed from this data by JMP. You need to use the *Distribution of Y* command from the *Analyze* menu to get these plots.

There are two ways to print the graphics. Both require that you know how to print files from a word processor. The two methods are to use the

- scissors tool to "cut" the pictures from *JMP* and "paste" them into your word processor file, or
- journal feature of *JMP* to record the steps of an analysis.

If you take the latter course, simply use the *Journal* command from the *Edit* menu to create a journal of the analysis. You can then save the journal in a variety of file formats, such as a Word for Windows file, which can then be edited using the associated word processor. The hard part of this assignment is learning how to use JMP and obtain printed copies of its graphs.

Assignment 1

You will need to download the data sets onto your own disk, according to the "Downloading Stat Data Sets for JMP" instructions to be passed out in class.

A1Q1. Fast-food outlets have a continuing problem with employee turnover. A district office for one chain obtained reasons for leaving for each of 216 part-time employees (mostly students) who quit over a 6-month period. Codes for reasons that employees quit are as follows:

> 1 = moving from area,
>
> 2 = time conflict with school work,
>
> 3 = new job with better hours,
>
> 4 = new job with better pay,
>
> 5 = conflict with other employees,
>
> 6 = conflict with supervisors,
>
> 7 = conflict with customers,
>
> 8 = inadequate pay,
>
> 9 = dislike of tasks,
>
> 10 = other.

a. Select the A1Q1.JMP data set using the *File* menu of *JMP*. Use the *Distribution of Y* command from the *Analysis* menu to obtain a summary of the reasons for quitting. From the chart, what ought this chain do to reduce the problem of employee turnover?

b. Obtain the mean, the median, and the standard deviation for "reason." What do these numbers mean in this context?

A1Q2. A mail-order clothing store must keep close track of the returns it gets from orders. Not only are returns expensive to process, but also they suggest loss of good will by customers. The store has a basic code for reasons for return:

> 1 = poor fit,
>
> 2 = don't like style,
>
> 3 = don't like construction (seams, buttonholes, etc.),
>
> 4 = don't like color,
>
> 5 = don't like fabric,
>
> 6 = item was mislabeled or wrong item sent.

The A1Q2.JMP data set contains the primary reason for the last 324 returns.

a. There is a perpetual three-way argument among store managers about returns. Purchasing is responsible for monitoring the design and manufacture of the clothing, marketing is responsible for conveying the nature of the clothing accurately, and shipping is responsible for filling orders precisely. Obtain a chart of the reason frequencies and use it to identify what seems to be the best area of opportunity for improvement.

b. The first 203 returns came from the spring catalog, the remainder from the summer catalog. Use the *Exclude* command from the *Rows* menu to subset the data. For each subset, obtain a histogram. Does there seem to be a shift in return pattern between the two catalogs?

A1Q3. As assistant to the president of a regional potato chip maker, you've been asked to analyze the results of a comparison of a national brand (coded as number 1 in the data set) to your brand (coded as 2). One part of the problem is the actual fill of nominal 16-ounce packages. One of the better ways to lose customers is to give them packages that don't contain the advertised amount. The A1Q3.JMP data contains actual weights of equal numbers of packages of the two brands.

Report briefly to the president as to how your brand (Brand 2) compares to the national brand (Brand 1); she can figure out averages herself, but requests your help in further analyzing the data. (The essence of this data comes from Ron Feuerstein; the data have been disguised to avoid libel suits, but they reflect Feuerstein's findings.)

A1Q4. National and international motel chains have toll-free reservation numbers. The waiting time between placing the call and obtaining a reservation agent is a major determinant of service quality. Long waits lose customers. One chain has a target that the average weight should be about 20 seconds. This target balances the annoyance felt by waiting customers with the high cost of keeping excess agents on duty. The chain's eight inspectors call the reservation number each day, recording the waiting time. The data for the last 30 days are in the A1Q4.JMP data set. Does the call waiting time meet the target? If not, in what way does it deviate from the goals?

A1Q5. A tool manufacturer sells masonry drill bits to contractors and homeowners. One critical dimension of bit quality is hardness. Too soft a bit causes rapid wearout; too hard a bit causes dangerous brittleness. The target value for hardness is 16.0 on a standard scale. Specifications allow a standard deviation of 0.5. Problems result from defective batches of metal and improper tempering in a furnace. Metal batches change every second day. Furnace problems evolve gradually, rather than going haywire suddenly. The A1Q5.JMP data set contains 5 hardness measures per day.

Obtain the average and the standard deviation for each day using the quality control charts. Are the produced drill bits meeting the standards? If not, in what way do they deviate from the goals?

A1Q6. A national parcel service must track the number of daily deliveries, looking for trends that indicate growth or decline as well as day-to-day variation. The A1Q6.JMP data set contains daily delivery numbers (millions) for the last three months of weekdays.

a. Obtain the mean, the median, and the standard deviation of the daily deliveries using the *Distribution of Y* command from the *Analyze* menu.

b. Use the *Overlay plots* command from the *Graph* menu to obtain a time sequence plot (connected or not, as you prefer) of the deliveries data. Are the data *stable*, without any evident trend? Are the data *random*, without any evident cycles?

c. Use the *New column* command from the *Cols* menu to add a new column named "Diffs" to the data set. Define the new column using a formula. Obtain the mean, median, and standard deviation of the day-to-day changes. How does the standard deviation of changes compare to the standard deviation of deliveries? Does this comparison indicate that yesterday's deliveries will be a useful predictor of today's deliveries?

Assignment 2

A2Q1. One way to test the quality of shock absorbers is to put them through a "torture test." Each day, a manufacturer attaches 8 shock absorbers to machines that simulate continuous severe bumps in a road. The number of bumps to failure (usually indicated by the shock absorber "bottoming out," occasionally by an actual break in the unit) is measured automatically. To be satisfactory, shocks should endure more than 40,000 bumps before failing. The A2Q1.JMP data set contains test data from 20 days; "btf" is bumps to failure, "daynumber" is just that.

a. Are the data stable, with no evident trend? Are the data random, with no evident cycles?

b. For the data considered as a single sample, can the manufacturer be confident that the mean btf is satisfactory?

A2Q2. Mutual fund managers are rated periodically on the net return per $100 invested. The A2Q2.JMP data set contains typical results, let's say for managers of balanced-growth funds. The yields are "return", and "fundnumber" is just alphabetical order.

a. Plot the return data in sequence (fundnumber) order, using the *Overlay plot* command from the *Graph* menu. Do you see a trend? Cycles?

b. Do the managers, on average, seem to beat the S&P500, which had a net yield of 8.34% in this period? How sure are you of your conclusion?

A2Q3. A chain of 10 home-improvement stores has a core list of 882 tools that should be available at each store. Every weekend, do-it-yourselfers descend on the store; occasionally, they run the store out of stock of a particular tool. Balancing the loss of goodwill of foiled customers against the cost of excess inventory, the chain manager has decided that ideally about 20 tool items will be out of stock at any one store by Sunday evening. An inspector visits one store each Sunday evening; among other duties, the inspector counts the number of stockouts. The data in A2Q3.JMP are "stockouts" and "storenum," for the last 30 weeks. Is the ideal stockout level being approximated?

Assignment 3

A3Q1. Wharton students are divided in their use of spreadsheet computer programs. Some use Lotus, others use Excel. A crucial variable in deciding which program is more effective is the time required to carry out a project. A staff member at Wharton Computing measured the total logged-on time for 100 Lotus projects and 100 Excel projects, both randomly chosen during April 1991; the only available information was the logged-on duration, short of interviewing users as they left. The A3Q1.JMP data set contains "duration" and "program" (1 = Lotus, 2 = Excel). Are there statistically detectable differences in durations between the two programs?

A3Q2. Sharply increasingly health-insurance costs lead to sharply increasing interest in controlling same. A benefits manager had the opportunity to assign employees to either a new, co-pay insurance policy or a variation of the existing policy. The manager used her judgment in deciding on which employees went to which policy. After six months, the total insurance-covered expense for each employee was determined. The A3Q2.JMP data set contains cost in dollars, and type of policy (1 = co-pay, 2 = current).

a. Does the evidence clearly indicate that there's any difference in cost results?

b. Do you have suggestions for how to conduct a follow-up study in a different branch of the company that's planned for next year?

A3Q3. Supermarkets send out cents-off coupons to attract customers, preferably high-spending customers. One market sent two different coupons to two ZIP codes near the market. The first ZIP code contained 12,600 homes, all of which received coupon 1; the second ZIP code (coupon 2) contained 11,800 homes. The supermarket was able to count the number of coupons used and the total amount purchased by each coupon user. The A3Q3.JMP data set contains "purchase" and "typecoupon." The store manager was interested in whether there were clear differences between coupons, and also in what could be expected if the coupon program were extended to many other, similar ZIP code areas. Use non-technical English to answer his questions.

A3Q4. Recently, several opticians introduced on-site labs that can prepare eyeglass lenses in one hour. Conventional opticians are skeptical of the accuracy of these labs. As a test, lens prescriptions of various (reasonably representative) types were randomly sent to on-site or conventional labs. The error in lens curvature was measured carefully. Of course, the target error is 0; negative errors indicate undercorrection, positive errors, overcorrection. Select the

A3Q4.JMP data set, which contains columns labeled "error" and "source" (1 = conventional, 2 = on-site). Obtain confidence intervals for the difference of means and for the ratio of standard deviations. Do the intervals indicate systematic differences between the on-site and conventional labs?

Appendix: Use with Minitab

Interested readers can reproduce the fundamental statistical content of the analyses in this book using Minitab in place of JMP-IN. This appendix briefly indicates the relevant features of the menu-driven, student version Minitab. Minitab can also be used in the now "old fashioned" command line mode. This mode of use is flexible and trains the user in the underlying programming language of Minitab. However, we suspect that this interface will become less common in introductory classes and have therefore focused on the menu-driven interface. The commands invoked via Minitab's menu generate the underlying typed commands of the older interface together with the associated numerical output in the Minitab session window. Also, we have only mentioned the commands that generate the so-called "professional" graphics in Minitab; character based graphics are also available.

While the statistical content (things like summary statistics and p-values) generated by Minitab will be identical to that from JMP-IN, the appearance and layout of the graphics will differ. These differences are generally unimportant and often a matter of taste. Although both packages share menu-driven, windows-based interfaces, the manner in which they are used differs. In particular, JMP-IN provides a graphical summary as part of the each analysis. We like this encouragement to look at the data. Minitab by-and-large separates commands which generate graphical output from those with numerical summaries.

Some features are of JMP-IN are not available in Minitab (and vice versa). The features of JMP-IN which are exploited in this book and its companion volume which are absent from the menu-driven commands of the student version of Minitab include

  • an unlimited number of spreadsheet cells for the data set,
  • kernel density estimates with interactive bandwidth control,
  • scatterplot smoothing,
  • leverage plots in regression,
  • logistic regression, and the
  • ability to temporarily exclude or hide observations in calculations and graphs
  (though they can be deleted from the data set)

The absence of these features will make it hard to follow every aspect of the examples, but are more inconvenient than crippling. The absence of the automatic leverage plots in regression is more serious given the graphical approach we have adopted. One can always generate leverage plots by hand (run two regressions and plot the residuals from each), but the required manual tedium will discourage all but the most curious students. It is hard to make up for the absence of logistic regression and one will be compelled to avoid these cases from the regression casebook without a suitable replacement. Of course, access to the full version of Minitab would remedy this problem since it includes logistic regression. We suspect that many, if not all, of these features will appear in Minitab in the near future. (We have not attempted to confirm this suspicion with the developers of Minitab.) Sophisticated users will doubtless be able to program some of these capabilities using Minitab's macro programming. However, the resulting commands will not be a part of the standard distribution and will not appear in the program menus.

Importing Data Files

The student version of Minitab limits the size of the data sheet to 3500 cells. In contrast, JMP-IN allows arbitrarily large data sets limited only by the amount of memory available on the user's system. This limitation of the student version of Minitab is adequate for most of the examples in this book, but will not accommodate all of the data used in the larger examples (such as Forbes94.jmp with 24,000 cells). Users who wish to use these large examples nonetheless can edit the associated data file to remove observations.

The first step in using Minitab with this book is to obtain text versions of the data sets. Minitab cannot read the JMP-format files used here, and you will need to obtain the "raw data". These raw data files (denoted by the suffix .dat rather than .jmp) are simply text files (ASCII files) with the data for the example arranged in a table with variable names listed in the first row. The initial part of the file name identifies the example from the book, as in Forbes94.dat. These files are available via the Internet from downloads pointer given by the URL

http: //www-stat.wharton.upenn.edu

A compressed archive contains all of the raw data files.

Once you have the data on your own PC, you can then import the desired data set into Minitab via the menu command

File > Import ASCII Data

Here, "File" denotes this menu item seen at the top of the Minitab window, and "Import ASCII Data" is an item in the associated drop-down list of commands. Choosing this command from the menu opens a dialog that you can complete to identify the appropriate file.

Descriptive Statistics

Commands offered by Minitab's statistics menu generate the needed univariate data summaries and those from the graph menu generate the associated figures.

Stat > Basic Statistics > Descriptive Statistics

Prints in the session window simple descriptive summaries, like the sample mean and standard deviation.

Graph > Boxplot
Graph > Histogram
Graph > Normal Plot

These commands produce the univariate boxplot, histogram and normal plot. The boxplot command also allows you to specify a categorical grouping variable so that you can see side-by-side boxplots (like those generated by JMP-IN's *Fit Y by X* command with a continuous Y variable and a categorical X variable). The normal plot is the normal quantile plot.

Graph > Plot

Generates a scatterplot of two variables.

Graph > Time Series Plot

Generates a sequence plot of one or more variables (corresponding to JMP-IN's overlay plot).

Two additional commands provide helpful summaries for categorical data.

Stat > Tables > Tally

Tabulates frequencies of a categorical variable.

Stat > Tables > Cross Tabulation

Shows the table of cell frequencies produced by two categorical variables.

Tests of Means, ANOVA

Stat > Basic Statistics > 1-Sample t
Stat > Basic Statistics > 2-Sample t

These commands do the one and two-sample t-tests based on comparisons of sample averages.

Stat > Nonparametrics > 1-Sample Wilcoxon
Stat > Nonparametrics > Mann-Whitney

These are the nonparametric alternatives to the two preceding mean-based tests.

Stat > ANOVA > Oneway
Stat > ANOVA > Twoway

These two commands generate one-way and two-way analyses of variance. Options allow the user to request additional comparison statistics, such as Tukey-Kramer comparisons.

Regression and Correlation

Stat > Basic Statistics > Covariance
Stat > Basic Statistics > Correlation

These two commands produce covariance and correlation matrices.

Graph > Matrix Plot

Generates a scatterplot matrix.

Stat > Regression > Fitted Line Plot

Shows a fitted regression line superimposed on a scatterplot of the underlying two variables. Optionally includes prediction confidence limits.

This command does not allow the user to superimpose fits based on various transformations of the data or polynomial models. Transformations of variables must be formed explicitly as new data columns using the Calc menu, with the associated fits plotted separately. For example, one can form a quadratic polynomial regression by first squaring the predictor and then adding this variable to the regression. We are unaware of how to show the associated regression fit with prediction limits using the built-in menu items.

Stat > Regression > Regression

Produces a regression analysis with options for additional graphical output (e.g., residual plots) and summary statistics (e.g., Durbin-Watson, VIF). Regression leverage plots for the predictors are not produced.

Categorical factors must be manually converted into dummy variables via the Calc > Make Indicator Variables command. Interactions must similarly be constructed before being adding to a regression model. Associated partial F-statistics must then be computed via fitting models with and without these items.

Control Charts

Stat > Control Charts > Xbar-S

Draws the X-bar and S (standard deviation) control charts together in one view. Other commands will also draw these separately.

Time Series Methods

In addition to the basic graphics and regression commands, Minitab offers an extensive set of time series tools. These include

Stat > Time Series > Decomposition

Automates the task of partitioning a time series into trend, seasonal and irregular components, with separate graphs summarizing each.

Stat > Time Series > Autocorrelation

Tables and graphs the lagged autocorrelations of a time series, avoiding manual calculations.

Stat > Time Series > Lag
Stat > Time Series > Difference

These transformations of data are located under the time series command item rather than as part of the Calc options.

Index